Greece and The West

Greece and The West

—

Theodore G. Karakostas

Other Books by Theodore G. Karakostas

In the Shadow of Hagia Sophia

With This Sign Conquer

Contents

How Did this Happen?

———

IN MY YOUNGER DAYS, WHEN I began as a student at Northeastern University in Boston, I developed a profound interest in political affairs and world history. Specifically I developed an interest in my Hellenic ancestry and the Hellenic homeland of my parents, an interest that was inseparable from the interest that I developed in my Orthodox Christian faith. I spent countless hours discussing with my father the brutal history of modern Greece, which included the Italian invasion of 1940, the subsequent Nazi occupation, and the military dictatorships that ruled Athens from 1967 to 1974.

It was in December of 1992 that I began reading a book that continues to disturb me to this day: *Smyrna 1922: The Destruction of a City*, by Marjorie Housepian Dobkin. The book describes an area of Greek history that is still not known by most of the general public in America and Europe: when the Ottoman Empire was divided in 1919, the great powers divided it up among themselves, and Greece was among those putting forth territorial claims.

Greece at the time was claiming territory that not only had ethnic Greek and Orthodox Christian majority populations but that also had been historically Greek. The American and European powers colluded against the Greeks to prevent a Hellenic victory against the Turks for economic reasons, and in the end over one hundred thousand Greeks and thirty thousand Armenians were slaughtered by the Turks in the ancient city of Smyrna in full view of American, British, Italian, and French warships, all of whom refused to intervene.

A very ugly story was told in this brilliant and well-researched book, which also offers an extensive bibliography. In 2000, I attended a lecture by the author in Brockton, Massachusetts, where she recounted her research and interviews with surviving witnesses. It is a disturbing and very troubling history and one that has had a tremendous impact on the formation of my political views over the subsequent years and inspired my devotion to the Hellenic cause.

Greece has had a troubled history over the decades. It experienced the horrors of Nazi occupation and mass poverty and suffering. During the years that I was studying and researching the history of Greece, things seemed better. Greece was then and remains for now a stable democratic republic, and economically at that time, in the eighties, Greece was certainly doing better.

The present economic crisis is a return to the very dark years of Greek history that preceded my generation. While I was in Greece between June 16 and July 10, 2015, the banks were closed. People were lined up in front of ATMs to withdraw sixty euros—the maximum that was permitted daily. In the absence of an agreement for a third bailout between the Greek government and the European Union (primarily the Germans) the crisis that began in 2010 worsened considerably.

Since the crisis began, there has been a rash of suicides in Greece by people who have despaired of the crisis. This is heartbreaking in an Orthodox Christian country whose faith sustained the nation during the long centuries under Ottoman Turkish rule. Seven or eight years ago, it would have been inconceivable to see homeless people on the streets of Athens, but today there are numerous homeless as a result of the crisis. On the other hand, there are also large numbers of homeless illegal immigrants who have made their way into Greece as a result of the misery emanating from the destructive wars of the Middle East and elsewhere that the West has been waging.

On July 24, 2015, the troika entered Greece to take control of Greece's finances. The troika consists of the International Monetary Fund (IMF), the European Commission (EC), and the European Central Bank (ECB). There is something obscene about this violation of the sovereignty of Greece, and this triggers memories of past meddling in Greek affairs by the Germans, British, and Americans.

One thing that Greeks can be thankful for is that they are not entirely friendless. Numerous media outlets and sources have expressed sympathy for the Greek plight. Most of them are leftist sources, but there are some conservative sources also. These include the *Economist*, who on its front page in July declared the subsequent acceptance by Athens of brutal austerity measures "a disastrous deal for Greece."

The July 13 issue of the *Telegraph* declared that "Greece is being treated like a hostile occupied state." Other more liberal commentators include Stephen Lendman, who wrote a commentary entitled "Banker Occupied Greece: Requiem for a Failed State." Andrew Gavin Marshall wrote "Blaming the Victim: Greece Is a Nation under Occupation," and Dr. Binoy Kampmark wrote "The Occupation of Greece: A Financial Coup d'État." These sources have expressed solidarity with Greece as a small and powerless country.

How did Greece go bankrupt? There are those who will say that Greeks are lazy and do not like to work (the German viewpoint). I will have much to say about the Germans in a later chapter. Several months ago the Organization for Economic Cooperation and Development made a study of the countries whose citizens work the most. They determined that Greeks ranked third as the hardest workers, after Koreans and Mexicans, but came in first among European countries.

The most legitimate criticism to be made of Greece is its corrupt politicians. The fact remains that Greek leaders are the worst. Apparently, the repeated borrowing over the years and decades brought on the economic crisis. This is not the fault of the ordinary Greek, who is forced to lose part of his or her pension. Nor are the Greek people at fault for what Greek leaders have done in secret.

I have been writing about Greece for twenty years. I started off writing letters to the editor in the midnineties and started submitting op-eds to Greek American newspapers. It was only in 2013 that I published my first book, *In the Shadow of Hagia Sophia*, followed by a second book, *With This Sign Conquer*, in 2014.

What follows is a critique of various fault lines regarding present-day Greece.

There are historical events in both modern Greek and Byzantine history that remain forgotten by Greek rulers and that should not be, such as the events of 1922 and 1923 that were touched upon in this preface and will be elaborated upon throughout this book. There will be a chapter on Greece's awful political leadership in recent history. There will be a chapter on Byzantium (which preceded the Ottoman Turkish conquests), which is necessary for an understanding of modern Greek identity and its tension with the West. There will be, of course, a chapter on Germany; it is due to that society's arrogance and brutal demands that austerity measures that have done nothing but torment the ordinary people of Greece continue to be imposed. There will also be a chapter on Russia.

This book is motivated by the many misconceptions of Greece being promoted by the worst elements in Western media. Thankfully, those elements appear to be in the minority. In any case, I am writing this because I believe in Greece and hope that what follows will be informative and of great interest to readers.

CHAPTER 1

This Should Not Be Happening

———

It is only with great trepidation that one can look upon events in Greece. The extent to which economic conditions in Greece have been permitted to deteriorate by Greece's political leadership over time is truly stupefying. This is what happens to a great nation whose leaders have lost their connections to their national honor, their citizens, their national rights, and their historical purpose.

It was George Santayana who said, "Those who do not remember the past are condemned to repeat it." Unfortunately, Greece is condemned to repeat history because Greek rulers have forgotten the history of Greece's foreign relations with the great powers.

All governments are obligated to defend the sovereignty, aspirations, and national rights of the people they represent.

They have an obligation to avoid a scenario in which their country is weakened to the extent that its existence is endangered. The responsibility of Greece's political leadership (and the blame lies with both the liberal Socialists and the conservative New Democracy) for the weakening of Greece is especially hideous and could have been avoided had not previous historical precedents been forgotten or disregarded.

In the preface, mention was made of events that transpired for Greece in 1922. It is this history that brings to mind the most obvious lesson that Greek leaders never learned. During the First World War, the Ottoman Empire began a murderous and genocidal campaign against the Christian minority populations that included Armenians, Assyrians, and Greeks. The Ottomans also aligned themselves with Germany, an alliance that alarmed Great Britain and France. This led the West to offer Greece territory in Asia Minor, such as the port city of Smyrna, which was populated by a Greek majority. Political events transpired in Greece that complicated events. The king of Greece, Constantine, rejected the offer, while Greece's prime minister, Eleutherios Venizelos (known as the Great Ruler, and rightfully so), perhaps the only genuine great statesman that modern Greece has produced, accepted the deal.

A national schism emerged, which resulted in 1920 in the downfall of Venizelos and the restoration of the exiled pro-German King Constantine in Greece, which led the great powers to abandon Greece by extending military support to the Turkish nationalists in Anatolia. There is no shortage of documentary evidence attesting to the inhumane policies adopted by the West toward Greece and the Greek populations of Asia Minor.

The American consul general to Smyrna, George Horton, wrote two letters to the State Department from Athens after the burning of the city of Smyrna by Turkish nationalists. He later wrote a book called *The Blight of Asia*, which traced how the United States, Great Britain, France, and Italy all adopted policies that were anti-Greek owing to various economic and political interests that were considered of greater importance than the aspirations of the Greek and Armenian Christian populations of Asia Minor.

Furthermore, Edward Hale Bierstadt, who was to lead the US Emergency Committee, which provided humanitarian relief to Greek and Armenian refugees, wrote a book harshly critical of American and European policies toward Greece and the Christians of Anatolia. His book, *The Great Betrayal*, condemned what it called "economic imperialism" that was conducted by the great powers. Likewise, American ambassador Henry Morgenthau would write a book called *I Was Sent to Athens* that also criticized the horrible mistreatment of Greece and the Christian refugees.

In 1923, the Treaty of Lausanne whitewashed the genocide of Christians under Turkish rule. The genocide of the Armenians, Assyrians, and Greeks during the First World War was deliberately forgotten. Furthermore, the Lausanne treaty called for an "exchange of populations" between Greece and Turkey. In reality, this was ethnic cleansing given legal sanction by the great powers, who had already demonstrated their anti-Greek animus when they permitted the slaughter of the Greeks at Smyrna and elsewhere in Asia Minor the previous year.

The Treaty of Lausanne oversaw the forcible uprooting of over one million Greeks from Asia Minor and Eastern Thrace. This included men, women, and children, who went on a long and dangerous exile all the way to Greece, which was documented by *National Geographic* in an article published in November 1925.

The racism against Greeks was best expressed by American admiral Mark Bristol, high commissioner at Constantinople, who stated that the Greeks are the "worst race in the Near East." Bristol has become infamous for his fanatical pro-Turkish, anti-Greek, and anti-Armenian stances. He discouraged reporters from adequately reporting on Turkish crimes and atrocities.

It is Lausanne and Smyrna that come to mind when considering the present predicament of Greece. The Greek government was friendless and paralyzed in 1923 when the Lausanne treaty was signed. Yet Greek leaders forgot this period in history. Greece has not fared well in history when it has been weak and vulnerable. Greece's leaders had an obligation to protect the country by ensuring that there would never be dark days such as those of 1922 ever again. But the concept of Greek interests is foreign to the politicians of Greece.

Another example of Greek leaders suffering from historical amnesia is the Council of Florence in 1439. In 1054, a schism erupted between the Greek Orthodox Church in Constantinople and the Roman Catholic Church. In 1204, the schism—which up to this time was theological—became political when the knights of the Fourth Crusade conquered and destroyed Constantinople while massacring its citizens and stealing its wealth and treasure.

In 1439, the Ottoman Turks were menacing Constantinople, and the Greeks were desperate. Emperor John Palaeologos traveled to Florence to discuss the possible reunion of the churches together with Greek Orthodox bishops and theologians. The pope insisted that there would be no move to help the Greeks until the churches were in full communion with one another.

Freedom of conscience is recognized by the civilized world as a basic human right. This includes theology and faith as much as it does politics. The West, through the pope, was essentially blackmailing the Greeks into abandoning their faith.

The Greeks at the time were compelled to accept Roman Catholic alterations to the original creed of the fourth century, which stated that the Holy Spirit proceeds from the Father alone, and not from the Father and the Son, as the Roman Catholics taught. The papacy also proclaimed itself to have primacy over all other bishops, a claim that conflicted with the Greek Orthodox stress on conciliarity, which emphasized that only decisions made by the Universal Church could be considered binding, not the declarations of one bishop. The Roman Catholics also insisted on belief in purgatory as well as the use of unleavened bread in Holy Communion.

The Council of Florence was an act of blackmail. Emperor John Palaeologos and the bishops and theologians who accompanied him became broken men and signed the agreement, abandoning their faith. A monk known as Saint Mark of Ephesus flat out refused to accept European bullying and became a hero among the people in Constantinople while the emperor and the unionists were denounced by the people for betraying the Orthodox Christian faith.

Ultimately, Constantinople fell in 1453. Despite the surrender at Florence, there was no real assistance emanating from the West. There were two thousand Roman Catholic soldiers from Genoa and Venice who went to fight alongside a small army of five thousand Greek soldiers against eighty thousand Ottoman Turkish soldiers.

As with the Lausanne treaty, the Council of Florence comes to mind amid the recent reports of tense Greek negotiations with Europe. This is another historical precedent that demonstrates how badly things end when Greece is at the mercy of the powerful. This should not be happening today. There are no better examples of how Greece's two major political parties have betrayed Greece by permitting the country to collapse into economic ruin.

CHAPTER 2

The History of the Surrender of Greek Sovereignty

———

EIGHT HUNDRED YEARS AGO, THE capital of Greece was Constantinople, and the Queen of Cities was the envy of the world. Religious fanatics in the West had developed an obsession with Jerusalem, and following the Muslim ruler Saladin's expulsion of the crusaders from Jerusalem in AD 1187, the West planned another crusade for the Holy City.

The treachery of Greek politics even then was notorious, with political factions vying for power and intriguing against one another. Alexios Angelus, son of the deposed Isaac Angelus, sought a way to take the throne of Constantinople for himself. The result was his journey to Western Europe, where he arranged to supply the Fourth Crusade with, as Steven Runciman writes, "military aid and large sums of money for the crusaders and money for the venetians." As it turned out, there were not sufficient funds available for Alexios to fulfill his promises. This is an early example of a Greek ruler willing to sacrifice his country's interests in the pursuit of personal power, and the outcome was the Frankish conquest of the city. In the year 1261, Michael Paleologos, who would usurp the throne of Constantinople and make himself emperor, liberated the great Christian capital from the crusaders who had conquered and occupied it in 1204. The Eastern Roman (Byzantine) Empire would never be the same. The conquest of the capital and decades of occupation led to the theft of the enormous wealth once possessed by Constantinople.

Once remarkably wealthy, Constantinople was broke following the liberation from the occupiers. Despite the expulsion of the Latin crusaders, threats were still made against the Greeks by the papacy. Emperor Michael, already condemned by the Greek Church because of his ordering the blinding of the rightful heir to the throne, came under pressure from the papacy to reunite the churches, which would be at the expense of Orthodox dogma.

The emperor undertook a prounion stance, angering his native Greek population and agreeing to the union of the churches (as his descendant John Paleologos would do in 1439) at Lyons in 1274. At the monastery of Zographou on Mount Athos, twenty-six monks were burned alive for rejecting the emperor's prounionist bullying.

The church question in Constantinople at this time was theological and political. The bullying of the Greeks by the papacy was a violation of both Greek sovereignty and religious freedom. A pattern was set for modern Greece that would be repeated after the completion of the Greek War of Independence.

Since the establishment of modern Greece following the successful War of Independence in 1833, there have been various forms of government in Greece. Greece has had a monarchy and military dictatorships, and it has been a republic at various times, all since the Second World War.

From 1945 to 1967, Greece was a monarchy, until it was succeeded by military dictatorships brought about by coups in 1967 and 1973. In 1974, a democratic republic was installed following the collapse of military rule.

Following the achievement of Greek independence and the formation of the modern Greek state in 1833—thanks in large part to the philhellenic activities of numerous educated people in America and Europe who admired classical Greek learning and philosophy—the great powers adopted a role as the "guarantors" of Greek independence. Great Britain, France, and Russia were theoretically all guarantor powers, but the Russians and their influence were minimized. Germany, on the other hand, played a major role in the newly established Greek state, as will be seen in a later chapter.

Greece was originally intended to be under the presidency of John Capodistrias, the former Russian foreign minister, but his assassination altered fate. Instead a monarchy was established in Greece under the rule of a Bavarian named Otho. Otho was a Roman Catholic with a Protestant wife, which contributed to the alienation of the Greek Orthodox Church in both Greece and Constantinople.

Otho's reign lasted from 1833 to 1862. His unpopularity led to his abdication after three decades of rule. His unpopularity had hit a high point in 1843, when a Greek revolt demanded greater constitutional rights and reforms.

In 1863, the Danish Glücksburgs became the new royal family of Greece under the reign of King George I, who would be assassinated after fifty years on the Greek throne. His successor would be his son Constantine, who would be the most destructive of the Danish kings. Constantine emerged in the same era as Prime Minister Eleutherios Venizelos, a Cretan who had fought for the unification of the island with Greece and who was a strong nationalist and Republican.

Venizelos, with his strong leadership and exceptional intelligence and abilities as a statesman and diplomat, exerted leadership over Greece during the Balkan Wars and presided over the liberation of Macedonia, Epirus, and Crete. Furthermore, Venizelos had his mind on unredeemed Greek territory in Asia Minor and Constantinople.

After the outbreak of the First World War, the Ottomans aligned themselves with the Germans, thus making compatible Greek interests with Great Britain and France.

The absurdity of the monarchy demonstrated itself by the conflict of interest in having a foreign dynasty rule over a country that it had absolutely no historical, cultural, national, or religious ties to (although, unlike Otho, the Glücksburgs did convert to Greek Orthodoxy when they arrived in Greece).

Venizelos saw the opportunity to strike against the Ottomans by accepting offers of an alliance with Great Britain and France. Constantine, however, who was related to the family of the German kaiser, rejected such an alliance. The conflict of interest was further exacerbated by the fact that the Germans were arming the Turks and assisted the persecutions and massacres of Christian Greeks, Armenians, and Assyrians.

The treachery by the monarchy in Greece can be seen by the fact that this family of foreigners had no connection to the Greeks who had endured centuries of persecution and enslavement under the Ottoman Empire before the uprising of 1821. Even more crucially, they had no connection to the Eastern Roman (Byzantine) Empire, which many Greeks—including this writer—still revere today.

The installation of a Danish-German family in Greece is an insult to the memory of the last emperor of Constantinople, Constantine Dragases Paleologos, who died in battle defending Constantinople on May 29, 1453. The only royalty who can morally or historically claim to be Greek royalty are those named Paleologos or Comnenos or any dynasty that ruled in Constantinople or the Empire of Trebizond, before the Turkish conquests. Furthermore, the traditional title of Greek kings is "Emperor of the Romans," not the bogus "King of the Hellenes" that the Glücksburgs used.

During the war, Great Britain and France offered Greece territorial rights in Asia Minor as well as Cyprus. Constantine turned down the offers as a result of his being related to the kaiser's family. Unlike the Danish king, Venizelos actively lamented the plight of the Greeks in Asia Minor who were being deported and massacred by the Turks. Venizelos said before the Greek Parliament, "it is not only the Turkish government that has a clearly outlined policy for the Extermination of the Greek race, a policy sufficiently demonstrated already against another race—the Armenians."

Over the short term, Venizelos prevailed when Constantine went into exile. In 1919 Venizelos put forward claims on behalf of the Greek nation in a memorandum that was submitted to the postwar peace conference in France. That document is entitled "Greece before the Peace Congress of

1919" and was published by the American Hellenic Society in 1919. Venizelos advocated not only the liberation of Greek populations but actively recounted the slaughter of Greeks, citing statistics in various cities and regions under Turkish control.

In 1920 Venizelos remarkably lost Greece's national elections. A referendum was held, and King Constantine was recalled after having been exiled. Constantine was considered to be persona non grata to the West, who never forgave him his pro-German stance. Originally his son, Prince Alexander Glücksburg, was to take the throne, but he died after being bitten by his pet monkey when he tried to break up a fight between another monkey and his dog.

As a result of this farce, Constantine was back in Athens, and the great powers betrayed Greece one by one. First the Italians made an agreement with Mustafa Kemal, followed soon by the French. Great Britain eventually stopped supporting the Greeks, and American business interests likewise colluded to undermine Greece's rights in Asia Minor.

The betrayal of Greece by Constantine does not in any way justify the atrocious actions of the great powers, who permitted the Turks to burn the city of Smyrna as well as to slaughter and forcefully expel the Greeks. Constantine's German connections and non-Greek ancestry do prove, however, that the monarchy was always a foreign plant and that what the Greek people had dreamed of for many centuries (the liberation of Constantinople that might have been achieved had Greece prevailed in Asia Minor) had been betrayed.

In 1924, not long after the appalling Treaty of Lausanne was signed, a republic was proclaimed in Greece by the military government that had seized power in 1922 by loyal Venizelist officers who were furious at the monarchy for its betrayal of Hellenism. The republic would last until 1935, when a Royalist prime minister, John Metaxas, with the full approval of King George II, son of Constantine, established a Fascist dictatorship. Disgracefully, Venizelos the only great man to rule Greece in the modern period, died in exile, was forbidden a state funeral in Athens, and was sent straight to his native Crete for burial.

The Glücksburgs went into exile following the German conquest of Greece, which followed the failed Italian invasion in which the leadership of John Metaxas was instrumental in crushing the Italians after their unprovoked invasion of October 28, 1940. After the German evacuation from Greece, British Prime Minister Winston Churchill supported the restoration of the monarchy. King George died and was replaced on the throne by his brother Paul and Paul's German-born wife, Frederika. The aftermath of the liberation of Greece from Nazi rule led to a civil war between Royalists on the one side and Communist insurgents on the other.

Frederika Glücksburg was the granddaughter of the German kaiser. According to journalist Peter Murtagh in his book *The Rape of Greece*, Frederika, while attending school in Austria, was in the female version of the Hitler Youth. Her uncle was also said to be associated with the Nazi SS, according to Murtagh.

From the viewpoint of a Greek nationalist and Orthodox Christian, this obscene woman's being considered Greek royalty is beyond infuriating. Later chapters will touch on the Eastern Roman (Byzantine) Empire and Greek nationalism, but something must be mentioned here with regard to the House of Glücksburg.

Some of the greatest women in Greek history were from the royal court of Constantinople—women such as Theodora, wife of the emperor, theologian, and saint Justinian; Saint Helen, mother of Constantine the Great; and Irene the Empress, who presided over the convening of the Seventh Ecumenical Council in 787, which upheld the veneration of icons in Orthodox Christianity by declaring that iconography was not idol worship: because God the Logos became flesh through the incarnation and entered human history, icons were permitted as aids in worshipping Jesus Christ.

In addition, there is the great Anna Komnena, daughter of Emperor Alexios Comnenos, who was one of the world's first female historians and a fine scholar who published an account of her father's reign on the throne of Constantinople that Byzantine historians still praise today, called *The Alexiad*. Frederica, referred to as the "ex-Nazi Queen" by the late journalist Christopher Hitchens in his book *Cyprus Hostage to History*, had no place being in Greece, much less attempting to usurp the legacy of the Greek Orthodox royalty of Constantinople.

A woman who wore a Nazi uniform, with its racist, pagan, and occult ideology, is a disgrace to Orthodox Greece. The example of this woman is yet another powerful argument against the Greek monarchy and a fitting illustration of the political corruption that has plagued Greece.

To Orthodox Greeks, Constantinople will always be the spiritual center. It is the city where the Ecumenical Patriarchate remains and where many sacred churches and shrines are located. In particular, the church of Hagia Sophia, the greatest of Greek churches, remains in Constantinople, although it is used as a secular museum.

In 1955, a pogrom was conducted by the Turkish government against the Greek Orthodox population of Constantinople. Members of the Greek community in Constantinople were beaten and raped, and their homes were burned and destroyed, along with their businesses and churches. In a single night, the entire Greek minority of Constantinople was made homeless.

In 1964, thousands of Greeks were deported from Turkey. In both these incidents there was not a protest from America or any NATO allies. The monarchy did not particularly seem to care about the outrages undertaken against the Greeks in Constantinople. Nor did the monarchy care for democracy in Greece, as can be seen by its blatant intervention in political affairs and hostility to any forms of political liberalization.

The monarchy was eventually abolished in 1974, when the Greek people voted in a referendum to abolish it. One major reason for the monarchy's abolition was the royal family's feuds over the years with Conservative Prime Minister Constantine Karamanlis (who resigned in 1963 as prime minister but returned to Greece in 1974 following the collapse of military dictatorship and made the decision to hold the referendum). The abolition of democracy in 1967 by the notorious colonels led eventually to the permanent demise of the monarchy. The royal family intervened in politics and feuded with Prime Minister Karamanlis, who would eventually be driven from office under pressure from the royal family.

Likewise, there were tensions between the monarchy and liberal Prime Minister George Papandreou, who replaced Karamanlis. In April 1967, a coup undertaken by three ambitious colonels overthrew democracy and installed a brutal dictatorship. It has long been believed that the coup plotters wanted to stop the foreseen electoral victory of George Papandreou in elections that were scheduled for May 1967.

King Constantine II, who inherited the throne when his father (Paul) died in 1965, swore in the junta leaders and was photographed with them. He was eventually exiled when a countercoup by Royalist generals failed to oust the colonels in December 1967. In 1974, Prime Minister Karamanlis, back in Greece for the first time since leaving the country in 1963, held the referendum that abolished the monarchy.

The military dictatorship—or junta, as it is referred to—became notorious for its use of torture against political dissidents. The junta tried to pass itself off as a nationalist movement, which it was not. Despite the slogan that it adopted for itself—"Greece of the Christian Greeks"—it was not a Greek Orthodox movement, either. It was simply a Western-backed dictatorship.

Greek Nationalism in modern Greece has been traditionally democratic. The leaders of the Greek War of Independence, which began on March 25, 1821, were nationalists who were inspired by the French and American Revolutions. The greatest example of the fusion between Greek nationalism and democracy or republicanism was the aforementioned Eleutherios Venizelos. Unlike the Greek dictatorship of 1967, Venizelos liberated unredeemed Greek territory during the Balkan Wars and came close to liberating

Greek population centers in Asia Minor, such as the coastal city of Smyrna.

Despite the achievements of Venizelos, the misconception continues that the military junta was a nationalist regime. The junta had its chance with Cyprus. The Republic of Cyprus was a small island that had achieved independence from Great Britain in 1960 as a result of the 1959 treaties of Zurich, London, and Guarantee.

Cyprus was 80 percent Greek, 18 percent Turkish, and 2 percent remaining minorities, including the Maronites and Armenians. Cyprus has been Hellenic going back to the classical period and was also part of the Eastern Roman (Byzantine) Empire. Cyprus came under Western rule for many centuries, was eventually conquered by the Ottomans, and was ceded to Great Britain in 1878.

In 1955, there arose a popular movement in Cyprus for *enosis* (union) with Greece, led by Greek Orthodox archbishop Makarios and Colonel George Grivas, who would found a movement called the National Organization of Cypriot Fighters (EOKA in Greek).

Great Britain urged the Turks to resist the Cypriot popular movement, and Great Britain and Turkey supported the Turkish minority against the Greek majority, who became the victims of terrorist attacks. In 1960, under enormous pressure and threats that Cyprus would be partitioned, Makarios accepted independence as the alternative to enosis. At the time, Makarios protested the constitution that had been drafted for the Republic of Cyprus and argued that the rights of the Greek majority were being undermined. His protests fell on deaf ears, including those of Prime Minister Karamanlis, who followed Western dictates for Cyprus.

President Makarios became disliked by the United States, Turkey, and the Greek junta owing to his insistence that Cyprus remain part of the nonaligned movement.

The military junta, so-called nationalists, advocated double enosis for Cyprus, meaning a division between Greece and Turkey. Makarios refused to countenance any plan that would divide Cyprus.

There was a slogan the "Greece of the Christian Greeks" used by the military junta. It has been stated from books of the era that the legitimate, or canonical, archbishop of Athens, Chrysostomos, was forced from his ecclesiastical office by the junta because he refused to swear in the leaders of the dictatorship. An anonymously written book translated by Richard Clogg, an English historian of modern Greek history, indicates that the archbishop and other bishops were purged because of their refusal to cooperate with the junta. There has long been a mistaken impression that the Orthodox Church of Greece supported the junta. This assertion was repeated by the late Philhellene Christopher Hitchens in his book *God Is Not Great.*

The fact is that the Greek Church was used as some sort of government ministry by the junta, which removed bishops it did not favor in complete violation of Orthodox canon law. Some bishops, on the other hand, did collaborate with the junta and willingly received their offices from them in violation of canon law and with total disregard for the trampled rights of their predecessors. This includes Archbishop Ieronymos Kotsonis, who was made archbishop of Athens by the junta. This archbishop had previously been an archimandrite, a celibate priest. In the Orthodox Church, priests have the option of marrying or remaining celibate. Celibate priests are called archimandrites and are eligible for elevation to the Episcopal hierarchy whereas married priests are not.

Ieronymos Kotsonis had not been a metropolitan (an Orthodox bishop) and did not have any of the experience or qualifications the members of the church hierarchy whom he surpassed had. The junta's interference with the church made a mockery of their claims to be Christian, as did their brutality and cruelty.

In November 1973, the junta used force against student demonstrators at the Polytechnic of Athens. Around twenty students were killed. In the aftermath of the turmoil, dictator

George Papadopoulos was overthrown and replaced by another army officer, Dimitrios Ioannides.

By the summer of 1974, conflict escalated between Athens and the Cyprus government of Makarios in Nicosia. On July 15, Athens ordered the assassination and overthrow of President Makarios, who survived. On July 20, using the coup as a pretext to achieve what it had always wanted, the Turkish government ordered the invasion of Cyprus.

Turkey had wanted the partition of Cyprus since 1955, when in Turkey a political party was formed called Cyprus Is Turkish. The anti-Greek pogroms in Constantinople were inspired by the collusion between Turkey and Great Britain, who sought to deprive the Greek Cypriots of their democratic and national rights to achieve self-determination by uniting with Greece. It should be emphasized that Turkey had renounced any and all claims to Cyprus at the conference in Lausanne in 1923.

Whereas the first Turkish invasion of Cyprus was limited to a small portion of Cypriot territory, a second invasion, on August 14, seized 37 percent of Cypriot territory and resulted in the ethnic cleansing of two hundred thousand Greek Cypriots and numerous war crimes against that community.

The Greek military dictatorship had collapsed on July 23, and elder statesman Karamanlis had returned to Greece.

Therefore, the Turkish invasion of August 14 exposed Turkey's aggression, expansionism, and war crimes against the people of Cyprus.

Constantine Karamanlis deserves credit for his leadership following the collapse of the military junta. He stabilized Greece by presiding over the first free national elections since the prejunta era, and, more importantly, he put the fate of the monarchy before the Greek people in a national referendum. In 1924, 70 percent of Greek voters had voted to abolish the monarchy; fifty years later, 69 percent favored its abolition.

Karamanlis founded the New Democracy Party that emerged from the ashes of dictatorship. Likewise, another political party, the Panhellenic Socialist Movement (PASOK) was formed by Andreas Papandreou, son of the late prime minister George Papandreou, whose probable election in May 1967 had been stopped by the military coup one month earlier. Karamanlis deserves credit for withdrawing from the military wing of NATO as a just response to Turkey's invasion of Cyprus. The Republic of Cyprus, a non-NATO member, was invaded by NATO member Turkey. NATO's silence to the invasion of Cyprus, like its previous silence toward the pogrom against the Greek population of Constantinople twenty years earlier, remains a contemptible example of hypocrisy and double standards.

In 1981, Andreas Papandreou was elected prime minister of Greece. He also pursued a nationalistic and independent Greek foreign policy. In 1985, he supported Cypriot president Spyros Kyprianos's rejection of a bad plan for Cyprus. In 1987, he threatened to sink a Turkish vessel in the Aegean when the latter sought to drill for oil in Greek territorial waters. In 1994, after having returned to power, Papandreou responded to Washington's anti-Greek policies on the issue of Macedonia by imposing an embargo on the former Yugoslav Republic of Macedonia.

Macedonia is a region of Northern Greece associated with Alexander the Great. The former Yugoslav Republic, with its capital in Skopje during the Communist era of former Yugoslavia, adopted the name of Macedonia as a means of claiming the region of Greece in order to pursue an outlet to the Aegean Sea. Skopje likewise usurped Macedonian symbols such as the ancient Vergina Sun, which it placed on its flag in 1992, and the White Tower of Thessaloniki (the capital of Macedonia), and its lunatic elements have distributed maps showing the region of Northern Greece as being part of its own territory.

The Clinton administration violated its promises to support Greece and recognized FYROM as Macedonia, thus provoking the Papandreou government into imposing an embargo when it closed the border with it in early 1994.

The acronym of FYROM stands for former Yugoslav republic of Macedonia, which was adopted as a temporary name in 1993.

Despite widespread criticism from its alleged allies, the Greek government held firm until an interim agreement in 1995, when Skopje agreed to change its flag and Athens lifted the embargo.

New Democracy returned to power under Prime Minister Constantine Mitsotakis between 1990 and 1993. As noted, Andreas Papandreou returned to power with PASOK in 1993. He would be removed as prime minister by his own party as a result of his declining health.

In January 1996, PASOK put into office its new leader, Costas Simitis. Simitis soon demonstrated his political ideals when he pursued policies of internationalism that were detrimental to the national interests of Greece. Simitis also demonstrated his hostility to all things Greek when, for example, he provoked a fight with the Greek Orthodox Church and Christodoulos, its charismatic archbishop.

Furthermore, the foreign policy of Simitis became a throwback to the pre-1974 era of Greece when foreign policy and national interests were pursued for the interests of the Western alliance rather than the Greeks. Among the numerous foreign policy changes carried out by the

Simitis government was the acceptance of the infamous Annan Plan, named for the former United Nations secretary general.

The Annan Plan would have blocked Greek Cypriot refugees from returning to their homes. Furthermore, the democratically elected government of Cyprus under President Tassos Papadopoulos rejected the plan, as did 76 percent of voters in the Republic of Cyprus. Simitis was joined by other Greek politicians, such as Foreign Minister George Papandreou (representing the third generation of the Papandreou dynasty) and others, in accepting a plan that the Cypriots themselves—who would be affected by it—unequivocally rejected.

The Simitis confrontation with the Greek Church will be discussed in the third chapter on Greek Orthodoxy. In 2004, New Democracy returned to power, with the nephew and namesake of Constantine Karamanlis becoming prime minister. This government was a welcome alternative to the PASOK government of Simitis and George Papandreou.

The Karamanlis government, despite coming under heavy pressure from the Bush administration, vetoed FYROM's candidacy to join NATO. Furthermore, the Karamanlis government behaved like a free and sovereign government by concluding an oil pipeline agreement with Russia and Bulgaria, one opposed by the Western European Union.

With the advent to power of the buffoon George Papandreou in 2009, the agreement with Russia was canceled. Papandreou was the West's man in Greece, much like his mentor Simitis. In 2002, Papandreou traveled to Ankara, Turkey, where he performed a Greek dance before his Turkish hosts—this in spite of the fact that Turkey has a history of genocide against Greeks in Asia Minor, Cyprus, and Constantinople and continues to be a threat to Greek airspace and territorial rights in the Aegean while occupying Cyprus.

It was during this period that the economic crisis in Greece was revealed. Greek governments had been borrowing too much. Greece returned to the horrible years of 1922 and 1923.

CHAPTER 3

Byzantium and the Greek Orthodox Church

———

DURING THE SPRING OF 2000, rallies were held in the cities of Athens and Thessaloniki to protest policies pursued by the prime minister, Costas Simitis. The rallies were called by the late archbishop of Athens and all Greece, Christodoulos. The purpose was to protest the removal of religion from identification cards in order to comply with demands made by the European Union.

Many objective onlookers might be forgiven if mistaken that the Greek Church was involving itself in politics or that the whole thing looked rather medieval from the perspective of secular Europe. However, there are various factors behind the two rallies that disprove the initial impression observed by Westerners.

In itself, the removal of religion from identity cards is really not a big issue, and had this been the only issue, there might not have been any real reason to rally the Greek faithful against the PASOK administration. The conflict between the Greek Orthodox Church and the Simitis government was nothing less than a confrontation between the Eastern Roman (Byzantine) heritage of Greece and the Westernization that has been imposed on Greece since the nineteenth century by the great powers.

For eleven centuries, the capital of the Greek-speaking world was Constantinople, which was established by Constantine the Great as a Christian city to replace Rome as the capital of the Roman Empire since the former capital had been associated with paganism. While the West was in the era of the Dark Ages, the Greek world flourished under the rule of the Christian emperor and the Greek Orthodox Church.

According to the late Sir Steven Runciman in his book *The Fall of Constantinople 1453*,

> For eleven hundred years there had stood on the Bosporus a city where The Intellect was admired and the learning and letters of the Classical Past were studied and preserved. Without the help of Byzantine commentators And scribes there is little that we would know today about the literature of

Ancient Greece. It was too, A City whose rulers down the centuries had Inspired and encouraged a school of art unparalleled in human History, an Art that rose from an Ever varying blend of the cool cerebral Greek sense Of the fitness of things and a deep religious sense that saw in works of art The Incarnation Of The Divine And The sanctification of matter. It was too, a Great cosmopolitan City, where along with merchandise ideas were freely Exchanged and whose citizens saw themselves not as a racial unit but as the Heirs of Greece and Rome, hallowed by the Christian faith.

Constantinople will forever be the greatest of all Christian cities, and the greatest of Greek cities. During these centuries, the Greek-speaking world was ruled not only by Constantine, but by the great Justinian, whose codification of law had a remarkable effect on Europe, and who was a theologian as well as the builder of Hagia Sophia in Constantinople and the Monastery of Saint Catherine on Mount Sinai.

Furthermore, the Eastern Roman (Byzantine) Empire saved all of Europe from the Arabs in AD 678 and AD 717 through the use of the instrument known as Greek fire, which was used to stop the Arab conquest of Constantinople and advance into Europe. The Greek world at this time was the center of Christianity, and the formation of Christian theology was shaped by church fathers such as Athanasius, Basil the Great, Cyril of Alexandria, Maximos the Confessor, and Saint John of Damascus.

As noted by Runciman, Byzantine iconography is remarkable and arguably proves the existence of God as a result of the word made flesh by its miraculous depiction of the heavenly realm and the glory of God. Furthermore, the Greeks preserved the texts of classical learning and literature at the universities of Constantinople. When the Greeks fled the empire in the years preceding the Ottoman conquest of Constantinople, they brought with them to Europe the manuscripts and texts of classical Greek learning. It was from these sources that the Renaissance would eventually be born.

During the eleven centuries of rule under the emperors of Constantinople, the Greeks were not only independent, but they also had a sense of purpose and greatness. The Greek monks Thessaloniki, Cyril, and Methodius would go on to convert the Slavs to Christianity, and eventually Emperor Basil II would be responsible for the conversion of the Russians to Christianity.

During the thirteenth century, the crusaders would attack and conquer Constantinople, and the Greeks would never recover. Since then, Greece has been at the mercy of the West. In 1439 came the infamous Council of Florence, and in 1453 Constantinople fell to the Ottomans. The last real Greek independent state, however, was the empire of Trebizond on the Black Sea, which fell in 1461. Following the conquest of Constantinople, the Ottoman sultan Mehmet II attempted to stabilize his empire by granting some limited autonomy to the Greek Orthodox Christians. He permitted a monk, scholar, and theologian by the name of George Scholarios to become Ecumenical Patriarch of Constantinople.

The sultan permitted the Greek Church to maintain some form of internal self-rule over its own flock. Baptisms, divorces, and marriages were internal matters of the Greeks and their church. However, the Ecumenical Patriarch was responsible for the collection of taxes and for guaranteeing that there would be no revolutionary activity against the sultan and his empire.

During the years of Ottoman rule over Greece, the Greeks and other Christian subjects would become increasingly oppressed. The Ottomans kidnapped Christian children from their families for recruitment into the Janissaries. The Janissaries were the elite fighting force of the Ottomans, fanatical jihadists indoctrinated and deprived of their national identity and Christian faith and turned into vicious fighting machines.

In addition, during the Ottoman centuries, legal disputes between Christians and Muslims were conducted in Islamic courts of law. Christians were required to wear distinctive forms of clothing and were frequently pressured to convert to Islam. New churches were not permitted to be built, and permission had to be obtained to repair damaged ones.

During these centuries, the Greek Orthodox Church became the protector of the faith and the preserver of national identity and the national conscience of the Greek nation. The Islamic rule of the Ottomans made no distinction between the secular and the religious. The Ottomans imposed their own model of political-religious rule on their Christian subjects.

The Greek Church was given a role that it had not desired or possessed during the long existence of the Eastern Roman (Byzantine) Empire.

Theoretically, the Ottomans recognized the Christian populations as *millets*, an autonomous nation or community, but in practice economic and political pressures were often exerted on Christian populations to convert to Islam, thus leading to the Turkification of the people. The Orthodox Church helped the Greek people maintain their national identity and the memory of who they were.

Unfortunately, many patriarchs and bishops become corrupt. At one point of Ottoman rule, the Phanariots, wealthy Greeks who took virtual control of the Ecumenical Patriarchate, controlled the church and thus exerted power over the Greek as well as other Orthodox Christian millets, such as the Serbs, Romanians, and Bulgarians. In many instances Greek bishops became corrupt because of their reliance on the local Turkish pashas (governors) for their authority and power.

Regardless of the corruption, the church on the whole protected the Greek nation and made it possible for Hellenism to endure until better days came along. Take, for example, the formation of the Philiki Etairea (Friendly Society) in the nineteenth century, which would spark the Greek War of Independence. An important way in which the national memory of the Greeks was preserved was through religion. The most important Greek church has always been Hagia Sophia in Constantinople. When Constantinople fell to the Ottomans, those who were in the church praying or hiding were slaughtered or carried off into slavery. The great church, which had hitherto been the cathedral of the Ecumenical Patriarch, was converted into a mosque.

Legends grew and tales were told to generations of Greek children of the priest who had been giving communion in Hagia Sophia until the Divine Liturgy was interrupted. The myth said that the walls of the great church were opened and the priest was pulled inside so that the Eucharist would not be profaned. It is said that the priest will return on the day that Hagia Sophia becomes a church once again to complete the liturgy.

Over the centuries, many pieces of music, works of literature, poems, and stories about the glorious Greek past centered on Constantinople and Hagia Sophia. Another tale tells of the memory of a great man whose sacrifice preceded the Ottoman conquest. Constantine Paleologos, last emperor of the Romans (i.e., Byzantines, meaning Greeks), died on the morning of May 29, 1453, resisting the Turks to the end.

Since Constantine's remains were never found, the legend grew that an angel came to him at the last minute and took him away and that he sleeps, awaiting the day when he shall be awakened and return to liberate his city. Of course, this is just a myth but a nationalist myth and a very moving one that helped remind the Greek people of their pre-Ottoman past. Patriarch Gennadios acceded to the demands of the Greek people to add Emperor Constantine Palaeologos to the list of saints in the Orthodox Church. In 1821, the Greek War of Independence was proclaimed on March 25, the Feast of the Annunciation of the Most Holy Theotokos (Mother of God). This was one of the most important feasts on the annual calendar of the Orthodox Church. It signifies the visitation to the Mother of God by the archangel Gabriel, who announced to her that she had been chosen to be the God bearer or Theotokos, Mother of God.

On that day, from the monastery of Agia Lavra in the Peloponese, it was Archbishop Germanos who raised the standard of revolt against the Ottoman Empire. In September 1821, the Greeks of Cyprus sought to join the revolt, and Archbishop Kyprianos—who supported the Greek fight—would be put to death.

Previous to the Cypriot archbishop's execution, it was the Ecumenical Patriarch Gregory V who was executed on Easter Sunday in front of the gate of the Ecumenical Patriarchate. This gate has not been opened since that horrible execution.

There is precedent for Orthodox primates taking such stands in favor of the people and their freedom. In the year AD 626, Emperor Heraclius was away from Constantinople when the great city came under assault from the Avars. It was the patriarch Sergius who, holding up an icon of the Mother of God, led a three-day vigil, asking for the intercession of the Mother of God to spare the city. The city was spared, and this was considered a miracle.

The Greek Orthodox Church has always shared in the suffering of the people. In the aftermath of the genocide of the Asia Minor Greeks in 1922, Archbishop Chrysostom of Smyrna was offered the opportunity to escape from the city before the nationalist armies of Mustafa Kemal conquered it. The following account comes from the American consul general to Smyrna, George Horton, in his book *The Blight of Asia*.

The tales vary as to the manner of Chrysostom's death, but the evidence is conclusive that he met his end at the hands of the Ottoman populace. A Turkish officer and two soldiers went to the offices of the Cathedral and took him to Nureddin Pasha, the Turkish commander in chief, who is said to have adopted the medieval plan of turning him over to the fanatical mob to work its will upon him. There is not sufficient proof of the veracity of this statement, but it is certain that he was killed by the mob. He was spat upon, his beard torn out by the roots, beaten, stabbed to death, and then dragged about the streets.

His only sin was that he was a patriotic and eloquent Greek who believed in the expansion of his race and worked to that end. He was offered a refuge in the French Consulate and an escort by French marines, but he refused, saying that it was his duty to remain with his flock. He said to me, "I am a shepherd and must stay with my flock."

He died a martyr and deserves the highest honors in the bestowal of the Greek Church and government. He merits the respect of all men and women to whom courage in the face of horrible death makes an appeal.

The story of Greek bishops protecting their Hellenic flock does not end there. During the Second World War, the Greek Church was led by the great archbishop Damaskinos. The International Raoul Wallenberg Foundation stated that the archbishop's public denunciation of the persecution of Greek Jews by the Nazis "is unique, as no document similar to the protest against the Nazis during World War II has come to light in any other European country."

Furthermore, the bishops of Zakynthos, Thessaloniki, and Volos have been properly honored for their efforts to protect Jews from the Holocaust. These bishops—Chrysostom of Zakynthos, Gennadios of Thessaloniki, and Joachim of Volos—have been listed in the Yad Vashem museum in Jerusalem as "righteous among the nations." In the aftermath of the infamous 1955 pogroms in Constantinople, where the Greek minority suffered horrendous violence in a single night and saw their churches, businesses, and homes destroyed or burned, the Western alliance stood silent, refusing to condemn the brutality of the Turkish government.

The Greek monarchy in power at the time was oblivious to the attacks on the Greeks, as was the Greek government of Prime Minister Karamanlis, which had just replaced the late premier, Alexander Papagos. According to Dr. Spyros Vryonis in *The Mechanism of Catastrophe*, about the infamous pogroms, the archbishop of Athens and all Greece, Spyridon, went on Greek radio to denounce not only the Turkish-backed pogroms but also the apathy of the United States, Great Britain, and NATO. Despite the efforts of the government in Athens to stifle criticisms of the United States and the West, the archbishop spoke his mind.

The Greek population of Constantinople had resided in that city since it was known as Byzantium. Settled by a Greek trader named Byzas in the seventh century BC, it had been the capital of the Greek Orthodox Empire for eleven centuries and maintained its status as a holy city for Orthodox Greeks. But the Greek minority would not survive under Turkish rule, as Turkey was a member state of the NATO alliance.

In light of the differing reactions to the 1955 anti-Greek pogroms, who can argue that the Orthodox Church of Greece is not the greater representative of the voice of the Greek nation, as opposed to the politicians of the entire political spectrum ranging from the Left to the Right? This brings us full circle back to the dispute between Archbishop Christodoulos and Prime Minister Simitis.

Archbishop Christodoulos was not meddling in partisan politics. Indeed, the Orthodox Church prohibits its clerics from holding partisan political office. The late archbishop was defending Greek sovereignty from the European Union, which was meddling in the internal affairs of Greece.

If Prime Minister Simitis wanted to bring about a policy of secularization, he should have brought it up for a national referendum. He should have started a dialogue with the Church of Greece or a national debate among the Greek public.

Was the removal of religion from identity cards going to lead to the removal of the cross from the Greek flag? Would icons and crosses be removed from public offices and schools?

Church-state relations in Greece are defined by the concept of *symphonia*, or harmony, established by Emperor Justinian the Great in the sixth century. This makes the church and the state partners. There should be no misunderstanding. Church and state are governed separately.

The Church seeks recognition that Orthodox Christianity is the faith of the Greek people. Christianity arrived in Greece during the first century. The travels of Saint Paul in Greek-speaking lands in Corinth, Athens, Thessaloniki, Cyprus, and Asia Minor are mentioned in the New Testament.

Every country has the right to its sovereignty, its traditions, its history, and its faith. The hostility of Prime Minister Simitis toward the Orthodox Church of Greece is unmistakable and constitutes his contempt and disdain for the sovereignty of Greece, as well as its people. The reader must understand that the Orthodox Church of Greece is the institution that has protected and served the nation, in contrast to Greek political rulers, most of whom have served the interests of the great powers rather than the interests of Greece.

Hostility toward the church from Greek politicians is an assault against Greek democracy for three specific reasons.

First, there has been an effort to purge Greece of its own history, a point made in the concluding chapter of *Greece: The Hidden Centuries* by David Brewer. The author refers to the way in which the Turkish burning of Smyrna was presented in schoolbooks for Greek students:

> Turkish historians have blamed the Greeks or the Armenians for starting the fire, but it was probably lit by the Turks and there is overwhelming evidence that they fed it by first spraying houses with petrol and then setting fire to them. But all the textbook has to say of the event is: "The Turkish Army enters Smyrna. Thousands of Greeks crowd at the port and try to leave for Greece." This seems to bland even for twelve year olds, and the critics were surely right to object to it.

Democracy respects learning and history. The attempt to deemphasize Greek suffering and the church's role during the dark centuries of Ottoman rule is an insult to democracy, as history is being distorted for political purposes. Secondly, Greeks have not been consulted on the matter. The Greeks have traditionally trusted the church, and they should have the right to debate church-state relations and have a say in what happens. Thirdly, the church is the voice of the people, as can be seen in the examples cited above. The effort to silence the church is nothing less than an effort to silence the voice of the Greek nation and people.

CHAPTER 4

Germany

————

THE BEGINNING OF THIS CHAPTER is an extension of the previous one, as it tells the story of the Greek Orthodox Church during the years that followed the establishment of the modern Greek state. This is a sad period for both the church and post-Ottoman Greece. The Germans, through King Otho and the Bavarian regency that was imposed on Greece, played a destructive role at the time.

In 1833, the modern Greek state was established, and in all fairness credit can and should be given to the Western powers Great Britain, France, and Germany for helping to recognize modern Greece (along with Russia). Also, credit should be given to the West as well for promoting liberal democracy and constitutionalism—in theory, at least.

The problem with the powers, however, is that they could not help themselves. They were not content to assist the Greeks in getting back on their feet after centuries under the Ottoman yoke. They began to meddle in Greek internal affairs, and that meddling continues today, taking the forms of NATO and the European Union.

Greece was initially intended to be a republic under the presidency of John Capodistrias, who, despite his Greek ancestry, had been foreign minister under the czar. Capodistrias was assassinated, however, in an act of madness and self-destruction that is all too characteristic of modern Hellenism. The great powers therefore decided that Greece should become a monarchy.

The first monarch of modern Greece was a sixteen-year-old Bavarian named Otho. Because of his age, a regency was required to assist him in governing the country. The regency consisted of three Germans: Colonel Heideck (considered because of his philhellenic sympathies), a lawyer named Georg von Maurer, and Count Joseph von Armansperg. There were several problems with these men.

The most obvious problem is that they were foreigners. A second problem is that Heideck and von Maurer were Protestants, while Armansperg was a Roman Catholic, as was King Otho. The very institution of the monarchy was foreign imposed, and that is why it would be overthrown once and for all in 1974.

There were three serious problems created by this situation. First, Greeks were being ruled by non-Greeks whom they had nothing in common with. Otho and his advisers had not participated in the Greek War of Independence. They had not made the sacrifices that Greeks had made for the war effort in terms of the shedding of blood and the misery that accompanies war. They had not experienced the centuries of oppression and demoralization that came with being ruled by the Ottoman Empire.

Secondly, Otho and his advisers were foreign to the traditions of the Eastern Roman (Byzantine) Empire. It is here that there would be an enormous clash with the rise of "the church question." Greeks had their own history that diverged from that of Western Europe. They also had their own interests that were not compatible with those of either their new German rulers or Western Europe in general.

Finally, the matter of the church question would emerge. Greece's Orthodox Christianity was different from that of the Western Christians who were now occupying the country that had only just been liberated from Ottoman rule. The Eastern Orthodox Church differs from the Roman Catholic Church in its structure. Whereas the Roman Catholic Church throughout the world is under the rule of the pope, who is considered infallible, the Orthodox Church consists of fourteen "local," or autocephalous (self-governing), churches, each with its own spiritual head known either as a patriarch, a metropolitan, or an archbishop.

There is a misconception among Orthodox Christians, including Greeks, that the Church of Greece in 1833 was carved out from the jurisdiction of its spiritual head, the Ecumenical Patriarchate, and established as autocephalous in order to eradicate Ottoman political influence in Greece.

This is a complete myth. The reality is that the new German rulers in Greece (with the backing of Great Britain) wanted to eradicate Greek opposition to the German king Otho and guarantee that Greece would not align itself with Orthodox Russia. The independence of the church therefore had to be curtailed in furtherance of the imposition of foreign rule in Greece.

A case could in fact have been made that leaving the Church of Greece under the Ecumenical Patriarchate of Constantinople would have left some Turkish influence in Greece. The fact remains, however, that this was a matter that should have been decided by the Greeks with the advice of the Russian government, which was the only great power that was Orthodox.

What happened was not the establishment of an auto-cephalous church for Greece, but the partition of the Greek Orthodox Church as if it were a political entity, with the Church of Greece coming under the heel of a non-Greek and non-Orthodox government in Athens. The blatant po-liticization of the church would be only one of the numerous political crimes perpetrated against "independent" Greece. Over thirty-five hundred Bavarian troops arrived to serve as part of the Greek army. The Greek fighters themselves who fought the War of Independence against the Turks were subsequently sidelined in the new Western order.

Among those who suffered in the new Western order were the old fighters of the Greek War of Independence. General Theodore Kolokotronis, the great hero of the War of Independence, ended up in a prison and was sentenced to death owing to his opposition to the tyranny that replaced the Ottoman tyranny.

According to Charles Frazee in *The Orthodox Church and Independent Greece, 1821–52*, Kolokotronis was the head of the Russian Party. In September 1833, Kolokotronis and his faction were arrested and put on trial for treason by the Germans. This would be like America being occupied by another country after the expulsion of the British and having George Washington arrested.

According to Christos Yannaras in *Orthodoxy and the West*, "In 1835 there were as many Bavarians as Greeks in the army and the gendarmerie." The whole government of liberated Greece was effectively Westernized and, more specifically, Germanized. It was a form of colonization of Greece that has continued, to both a greater and a lesser extent, up to the present time.

There is something to be said about the narcissism and arrogance of Western imperialism. Certainly it would be unfair to condemn the great powers entirely. Many of the English and Germans active in Greece were philhellenes who supported the War of Independence and admired classical Greece. However, they did not understand the Greek people and their aspirations, nor did they understand that Greece had national interests and aspirations entirely distinct from their own.

The most effective means that the Western colonizers of Greece used to subjugate Greece was to strike at the church, the heart of Hellenic identity and nationhood.

When the church question arose, John Kapodistrias, the first Greek president (before he was assassinated), advocated autocephaly for the Church of Greece, meaning self-government, with the local church electing its own bishops and governing its own affairs. Under this pretext, a wholesale anti-Orthodox purge was instituted in the territory of liberated Greece.

Czar Nicholas I of Russia had taken the position that the sovereign of Greece should be Orthodox. The Russians understood the Greeks much better than the West did because of their shared Orthodox faith and Eastern Roman (Byzantine) heritage.

The Russians were overruled, and the likes of Georg van Maurer and the others acting on behalf of the young king

adopted policies toward the church that could only be charac-
terized as sacrilegious. According to Christos Yannaras, "To
fund the construction of the Athens cathedral, seventy-two
byzantine or later churches were demolished and the sites
sold. Many of these Churches were of great architectural
merit with wonderful frescoes." The Byzantine heritage is
widely praised and honored by scholars and historians. In recent decades, Byzantine art and iconography have been dis-
played at the Metropolitan Museum of Art in New York and
elsewhere. The destruction of Byzantine churches in Greece
by the German regency is both blasphemous and an assault
on sites that would likely today be classified as world heritage
sites.

For political purposes, then, historic Greek churches
that survived the four-centuries-long subjugation under the
Ottoman Empire were destroyed by the allegedly enlightened
rulers from Western Europe. There was a huge division between the European rulers of Greece and the Orthodox clergy
whose predecessors preserved the faith and the national consciousness of the Greek people. The bishops and priests wished
to remain with the "mother church" of Constantinople, while
the Bavarians opposed it. Political lines therefore were drawn
along religious ones.

Prominent theologians objected to the subjugation of the
church by the Germans. Two bishops who had supported the
Greek War of Independence, Ioannikios of Rethymnon and

Gerasimos of Adrianople, returned to Constantinople owing to disillusionment caused by the European colonization of Greece.

Georg von Maurer took an aggressive anti-Russian stance. He wanted Greece purged of all Russian influence. Furthermore, in violation of both Orthodox canon law and Greece's Byzantine heritage, his vision of church-state relations for Greece was modeled on the Lutheran Church in Germany. The Russian envoy in Greece strongly opposed the violation of the Greek Church's rights.

The Bavarian occupiers then waged a war against Greek monasteries. Over 412 monasteries were closed, and the government installed by the foreign occupiers seized their properties. The bishops also came under the power of the state.

According to Charles Frazee, "It was not lost on the regents that the monks were more opposed than any other group in Greece to the church settlement." He goes on to say that the monks were "the most vigorous partisans of Russia." We can see that the church was the voice of freedom in Greece that had to be silenced by the colonizers.

Between 1833 and 1852, there would be no less than fifteen uprisings throughout Greece as a result of the imposition of foreign colonial rule, which remains in place today under the guise of NATO and the European Union. It is very important for the reader to understand that the role played by Orthodox clerics and monks had nothing to do with theocracy or a thirst for power. Rather it emerged from the simple desire for freedom of religion and a nationalistic desire to defend the sovereignty of Greece against the imposition of the foreigners.

According to Christos Yannaras, three such clerics and theologians were Konstantinos Oekonomos, Christophoros Panagiatopoulos, and the theologian Kosmas Phlamiatos. Panagiatopoulos, also known as Papoulakos, was a monk who heroically preached against the desecrations against Orthodoxy and for the freedom of Greece. It is from this tradition that Archbishop Christodoulos would emerge. Further antagonizing the church, the Bavarian regency printed copies of the Old Testament from the Hebrew rather than the Septuagint version that is officially used by the Eastern Orthodox Church. The Septuagint version of the Old Testament is a Greek version of the original Hebrew that was translated by Hellenistic Jews around 300–200 BC. The opposition by the church and its supporters to defend itself and the nation against the blatant interventions in the internal affairs of both church and state were manifestations of popular sentiment for democracy and national sovereignty. The ultimate expression of this movement occurred in September of 1843, when a revolution led by Colonel Demetrios Kallergis forced the Bavarian king to expel his German advisers, who were replaced with native

Greeks, and to agree to provide a constitution for Greece. The military uprising should have gone farther and abolished the monarchy altogether. In 1850 the Ecumenical Patriarch of Constantinople formally recognized the autocephaly of the Orthodox Church of Greece. The relations between the Church of Greece and the Ecumenical Patriarchate improved, but some tensions still exist today.

The establishment of the Bavarian regency under King Otho serves as only one example of the difficult experience that Greece has had with Germany. More difficulties were to erupt during the First World War. During the period of that war, the Ottoman Empire and the Germans were allies, and during the war, the Ottoman Turks saw the opportunity to effectively deal with the Armenian, Assyrian, and Greek Christian populations that they considered to be trouble. The solution was genocide.

In 1918, the American Hellenic Society published a document, "Persecutions of the Greeks in Turkey Since the Beginning of the European War." In this document, an interview between the Greek chargé d'affaires in Berlin and the German foreign minister is cited, in which the latter states that the Greek population under Ottoman Turkish rule is a threat to the Ottomans. Furthermore, in Germany the press was censored, and atrocities against the Greek, Armenian, and Assyrian Christians were omitted from publication.

In 1926, a book entitled *The Blight of Asia* was published by the former American consul general to Smyrna, George Horton, who was America's diplomat in that city between 1911 and 1922. Commenting on the German-Ottoman alliance and the policies toward the Christians under the Turks, Horton wrote, "In fact there is little doubt that Germany inspired the expulsion of the Ottoman Greeks of Asia Minor at that time, as one of the preliminary moves in the war, which she was preparing."

A recent book entitled *Ataturk in the Nazi Imagination*, by Stefan Ihrig, includes research from newspapers during the early period of the Nazi Party, many years before its ascension to power. According to Ihrig, "The Christian minorities, particularly the Greeks and Armenians, were presented as a fifth column and the Greek 'terror' was especially highlighted in the article."

Much evidence is provided in Ihrig's book that the German Nazi Party admired the Turks and the future dictator Mustafa Kemal while expressing disdain for Greeks and Armenians, whom the German Nazis considered the equivalent of Jews in Turkey. Finally, according to the American Hellenic Society, "The Germans in June 1915, were aware of the decisions of the Young Turk Committee." These decisions included the stripping of the rights of Greeks in the Ottoman Empire and "the Turkification of the Greek element by force."

The genocide of the Greek population of Asia Minor was completed later when the successors to the Young Turks, led by Mustafa Kemal Pasha, conquered the city of Smyrna in September 1922 and slaughtered that city's Greek and Armenian populations. The genocide, however, had begun earlier, in 1914, as has been shown by the afore-mentioned sources cited, and with the active support of the Germans.

In his recent book, *The Great Fire*, about the Turkish destruction of Smyrna, Lou Ureneck wrote about the Germans during the First World War: "At the urging of Germany, the Ottoman government stepped up its campaign to remove ethnic Greeks from Western Anatolia. Turkish terror drove nearly two hundred thousand Greeks out of the country to the Aegean islands or mainland Greece."

The historical events, however, that are most remembered by Greeks that pertain to the Germans are the horrors experienced during the Nazi occupation of Greece. Greece at the time was ruled by Fascist Prime Minister John Metaxas, who, on October 28, 1940, received an ultimatum from the Italian ambassador, demanding the right of Italian troops to pass through Greek soil. The response of Metaxas was the famous "Ohi," meaning no. The Italian troops that had invaded Greece from occupied Albania were effectively crushed and humiliated in only ten days and were pushed back to Albania.

In response, Hitler felt the need to save his Italian ally, and so in April of 1941, Nazi Germany conquered Greece and installed a puppet collaborationist government. Prime Minister Metaxas had passed away in January 1941 and would have fiercely resisted the Germans, as he had the Italians. The Nazi occupation was brutal and led to the starvation as well as massacre of Greek civilians.

One of the most notorious massacres took place on August 16, 1943. According to Mark Mazower in *Inside Hitler's Greece*, 317 villagers were slaughtered by the Germans on this date. The victims ranged from a one-year-old girl to a seventy-five-year-old woman. Mazower notes that twenty families in their entirety were murdered and seventy-four children under the age of ten were among the victims.

Mazower's thorough research includes details about an SS camp that was established at a place outside Athens called Haidari. On May 1, 1944, over two hundred Greeks were shot in cold blood. This particular camp became notorious, and the Germans wanted its infamous reputation to be known in order to deter resistance to the occupation. In addition to the executions, torture was practiced; prisoners were beaten and whipped.

In the town of Kalavryta in October 1943, the entire male population was shot. One Nazi officer, General Karl von Le Suire, became notorious for the savagery of his troops, who burned over twenty-five villages and shot nearly seven hundred Greeks.

Mark Mazower writes about the scarcity of food in Greece during the German occupation and the famine caused by the war: "In Berlin, however, The Ministry of Food and Agriculture was against giving any assistance to Greece at all." Furthermore, (Foreign Minister) Ribbentrop at the Foreign Ministry declared that there were no pressing foreign reasons to worry about Greece at the Reich's expense." Hermann Goering, number two man in the Third Reich, stated that "if food supplies were to be sent anywhere in occupied Europe, Belgium, Holland, and Norway should receive priority over Greece." The Greeks therefore were condemned to starve during the war from the famine brought about by the occupation and the theft of the country's resources.

In addition to the horrors of famine and massacres perpetrated against the people of Greece by the Germans, the occupiers likewise sought to steal the country's cultural and religious treasures. One such attempt thankfully ended in failure, when German academics traveled to Mount Athos, with its twenty Eastern Orthodox monasteries and their numerous treasures.

German academics acting on behalf of the Third Reich visited the monasteries and catalogued the religious treasures, including icons and relics, with the aim of eventually stealing them. Thankfully, the monasteries survived untouched by the Nazi savagery. The believer in me attributes this spiritual victory to the power of the Theotokos (Mother of God), considered the protector of the Holy Mountain and its monasteries against the satanic and pagan ideology of the German barbarians.

When discussing the German occupation of Greece, one must of course mention the horrific fate of Greece's Jews. The Jewish community of Greece is one of Europe's oldest Jewish communities. Despite the best efforts of the Greek Orthodox community, the Nazis deported most of Greece's Jews to the death camps.

Distinguished opponents of the Nazis' "final solution" included Damaskinos, the Greek Orthodox archbishop of Athens, and several metropolitans, including Gennadios of Thessaloniki, Ioacheim of Volos, and Chrysostom of Zakynthos.

SS General Stroop, who had previously and with great cruelty put down the Warsaw Ghetto Uprising by the Jewish resisters, was transferred to Greece, where he was confronted by Archbishop Damaskinos of Athens and twenty Greek intellectuals who signed the archbishop's letter of protest against the deportation of Greek Jews. A document published by Hephaestus Books on "Eastern Orthodox Righteous among the Nations" refers to the letter by Greece's top cleric by asserting, "According To the International Raoul Wallenberg Foundation the Appeal of Damaskinos and his fellow Greeks is unique as no document similar To the protest against the Nazis during World War II has come to light in any Other European Country."

According to Kyriakos C. Markides in *The Mountain of Silence*, "It was during the Nazi occupation that a number of Greek Jewish women and their children found refuge on the Holy Mountain. The Athonite Fathers hid them there for the Entire Duration of Nazi Rule." Mount Athos, or the Autonomous Monastic State of the Holy Mountain, is dedicated to the Mother of God, and since females are not worthy of her, females are banned from the Holy Mountain. While Mount Athos is conservative and traditionalist, it remains a hotbed of Christian and Hellenic hospitality, as can be seen by the protection granted to Greek women and children of Jewish faith.

The chapter on Germany has been a historical review in the intervention of Greek internal affairs by the Germans and by the destructive policies and actions conducted by them in their foreign policy during the First World War and later during the occupation of Greece in the Second World War. The main reason for including these historical recollections is to expose the blatant hatred directed against Greece in the aftermath of that country's economic collapse.

The Germans are depicted by some media sources as the responsible Western country in contrast to the lazy Greeks who refuse to make sacrifices to salvage their economy. The truth is that Germany's past makes that country completely unfit to adopt a posture of self-righteousness. The Germans have never paid reparations for the horrors they inflicted on Greece during the Nazi occupation.

Accusations of laziness aimed at the Greeks sound rather hollow from people who seek to minimize their historical crimes. Likewise after the Second World War, German debts to victims among European countries were forgiven. The Greek government was among those that extended mercy and forgiveness to the Germans.

It is not fair to hold the present generation of Germans responsible for the crimes of previous generations, but it is quite reasonable to suggest that they humble themselves in light of their history. Even before Hitler's occupation, the Germans assisted the Ottomans while the latter were perpetrating genocide against the Greeks, as well as the Armenians and Assyrians.

People can say what they like about the Greeks in light of the present economic problems, but in response, those of us of Greek ancestry are very much entitled to remind the Germans of their own imperfections. The Nazi-orchestrated holocaust of the Jewish population of Europe was perpetrated by sophisticated and educated Germans. Josef Mengele and other sadistic psychopaths were physicians and were very well educated.

The question always asked by scholars and academics is how a civilized country could have conceived Auschwitz and Treblinka. The theologian in me will respond by saying that all humans are capable of good and evil. The behavior of the Germans during the Nazi era should destroy the illusion that some members of humanity are civilized and others are not. The Germans should get off their high horse.

The Germans should be more flexible with regard to Greece. One of the accusations against Greeks made by right-wing demagogues is that the Greeks want other people's money, in particular the money of the hardworking Germans. What Greeks actually want is relief and mercy—something the Allies extended to the Germans after Hitler's regime caused the deaths of fifty million people.

CHAPTER 5

Russia

———

GREEK RELATIONS WITH RUSSIA ARE over one thousand years old, dating back to the year AD 988, when Kievan Rus was Christianized by the Greek Empire at Constantinople by an arrangement of Emperor Basil II. Prince Vladimir of Kiev accepted the Christian faith as part of an arrangement with the emperor of Constantinople, who agreed for his sister to become Vladimir's bride. Over the course of time, as the Eastern Roman (Byzantine) Empire was weakened, Russia grew in stature and strength.

From AD 988 until AD 1448, the metropolitan of Kiev, who was the spiritual leader of the Orthodox Russians, was a Greek appointed by the Ecumenical Patriarch of Constantinople. In response to the Greek capitulation at the Council of Florence in 1439, the Russians finally declared their church autocephalous and self-governing, as the Greeks under Emperor John Palaeologos were considered to have abandoned the Orthodox faith along with the bishops who signed the documents at Florence. In 1453, Constantinople fell to the Ottoman Turks after a heroic resistance that finally collapsed after a fifty-seven-day siege of the city.

In 1472, Sophia Paleologos, the niece of the last emperor, was married to Czar Ivan III. According to the great Russian writer Fyodor Dostoevsky, it was under Ivan III that Russia began to display the Byzantine two-headed eagle. The two-headed eagle originated under the emperors of Constantinople, and the two heads facing east and west symbolize the meeting point of Europe and Asia at the Bosporus.

In 1589, Ecumenical Patriarch Jeremias II of Constantinople paid a visit to Russia, where he was received and honored by Czar Feodor. According to the late scholar Steven Runciman in *The Great Church in Captivity*, the czar sought recognition for the Russian church's autocephaly and for the rank of being a patriarchate. The czar asked for Moscow to rank third among the patriarchates (behind Constantinople and Alexandria), but the Ecumenical Patriarch insisted that Moscow would rank fifth, under Antioch and Jerusalem as well.

To this day, the Russian Patriarchate of Moscow ranks fifth among Orthodox Churches. Runciman writes, "Jeremias thus makes it clear that he recognizes Russia's claim to be the third Rome politically but not Ecclesiastically." Further on,

Runciman adds, "It provided the Orthodox with a Powerful lay protector in terms sufficiently flattering for the protector to abandon Greater Ecclesiastical Claims."

As such, the only surviving official of the Eastern Roman (Byzantine) Empire gave his blessing to the Russian czar to become protector of Orthodox Christians just as his predecessors in Constantinople had once been. In later centuries, Russia sought to protect the Christians of the Ottoman Empire, much as Russia is today attempting to protect the Christians in Syria.

An interesting example in the development of Greek-Russian relations comes from Catherine the Great, who ruled Russia from 1762 to 1796. Catherine was interested in establishing what was known as the "Greek project," which necessitated the establishment of a Greek state from the Ottoman Empire with its capital at Constantinople. This never happened, but Catherine's armies waged war against the Ottomans in 1774 in the Battle of Kachuk Kainarji, which forced the Ottomans to grant equal rights to Christians in the Ottoman Empire.

Great Britain believed its interests were in keeping the Russians out of the Near East. With India as part of the British Empire, London worried about its routes to India. Along with France, the British believed their interests lay in the preservation of the Ottoman Empire, even as Russian officials in the nineteenth century referred to the Ottoman Empire as the "sick man of Europe."

In 1853, the Crimean War broke out, and what is particularly interesting is that the roots of this conflict lay in the feud between Greek Orthodox and Roman Catholic monks over the holy shrines in the Holy Land, which was under Ottoman rule. The French encouraged their own monks to make claims to the holy shrines. These claims were violently resisted by the Greek monks, and soon enough Russia joined in the conflict as protector to the Orthodox.

With the war widening to include geostrategic interests, the Russians could have liberated Constantinople and the Christians of the Ottoman Empire, but the great powers of the West supported the Ottoman Empire. According to Orlando Figis in *The Crimean War*, the British even sang an odious song, "The Russians Shall Not Have Constantinople."

Greece wanted to enter the war under King Otho, but Great Britain and France occupied the port of Piraeus to show the Greeks their place. Greece naturally was sympathetic to the Russians. The Russians were the protectors of Christians in the Ottoman Empire.

Greece's ties with Russia are natural, brought about by a shared Orthodox faith. It has always been a mistake on the part of the West to interfere with that natural relationship.

Greek sympathy for the Russians can be further explained by the fact that the Ottoman Empire was oppressive not only to Christians in general but specifically to the unredeemed Greeks who desired to be united with Greece.

Great Britain and France betrayed the Christian populations of the Ottoman Empire by continuing to prop up and protect the Ottomans. They were suspicious of Russian expansionism but failed to recognize Russia's legitimate right to protect Christians. Following the conclusion of the Crimean War, the Russians were forced to renounce the right to protect Christians in the Ottoman Empire, a right that had been earned by Catherine's military victories in 1774.

At the time of this writing, there are tensions between Russia and the West over Moscow's presence in Syria. Russian motivations have been inspired in large part by concerns of the Russian Orthodox Church for the Christians of Syria. The Christians of Syria, like those of Iraq, are suffering genocide as the result of the policies of regime change instituted by the West. The United States today, like Great Britain and France in earlier centuries, has not taken into consideration the plight of Christians in the Middle East. The same reflexive Russophobia is at work today in the aftermath of the shooting down of a Russian plane by Turkey.

One of the ambitions of Russia was to liberate Constantinople, which is to Greek Orthodoxy what Rome is to Roman Catholicism. In previous centuries, the Greek and other Christian populations represented a significant proportion of the population in that city, perhaps a majority.

In any case, the Russians were officially granted Constantinople by the Western powers in 1915 through a secret agreement. The Russian Revolution of 1917 eventually changed everything, with Lenin renouncing the agreements. In 1955, the Turkish government orchestrated the infamous anti-Greek pogrom, which led to the destruction of the Greek community in that city. Not a single criticism of support for Greece emanated from any NATO country. The archbishop of Athens, Spyridon, at the time went on Greek radio to condemn not only the Turks but also the sinister apathy of the Western powers. The archbishop noted that if there had been a Christian government in Russia, the Turks would not have instigated the pogrom. The Archbishop's references to Russia recall the days of the Ottoman era when the Greeks looked to the Russians for support.

In 2002, United Nations Secretary General Kofi Annan conceived of a plan for Cyprus that was rejected in an April 2004 referendum by the citizens of the free Republic of Cyprus. Nearly 80 percent voted against the plan, as did the democratically elected president, Tassos Papadopoulos. Despite this, the Bush administration and Blair government in Great Britain supported the Annan Plan, which would

have solidified the Turkish occupation of the northern territories of Cyprus.

In 2004, Kofi Annan with the support of the United
States and Great Britain sought to make this racist plan that
would have denied freedom of movement and other basic
rights to the Greek Cypriots as the official basis for a settlement at the United Nations Security Council. After an appeal
by the Greek Orthodox archbishop of Cyprus to President
Vladimir Putin of Russia, the Russian ambassador to the
Security Council vetoed the plan. This was a rare victory for
Greek interests. In 2013, the Greek Orthodox archbishop of
Athens traveled to Moscow to collect funds from the Russian
Orthodox Church, which had raised donations from generous Russian Christians throughout Russia for Greeks hurt by
the crisis.

The Russians have been very generous to the Greeks and
supportive while the West bullies Greece, and if Athens tries
to undertake a foreign-policy initiative in accordance with
its own interests that enable it to cooperate with Moscow,
Greece comes under pressure. This occurred when Athens
sought to establish an agreement with Moscow over an oil
pipeline.

In November 2015, the Turkish government nearly
triggered a third world war when it recklessly ordered the
shooting down of a Russian plane over Syria. The Obama

administration, NATO, and the European Union failed to find fault with Turkey.

As in previous centuries, Russia took military action to protect Christian populations in Syria from the Islamic State. As with its Ottoman forebears, the regime in Turkey was saved from its disastrous actions by the West. In the aftermath of the Turkish aggression, Russian parliamentarians suggested that the crisis could be defused if Turkey permitted the great church of Hagia Sophia (now a museum) to be restored as an Orthodox cathedral, with Russia paying for the restoration work.

CHAPTER 6

Hellenism, Orthodoxy and Democracy

———

THE FUTURE OF GREECE DEPENDS on three important elements that together can and should serve to unify and stabilize Greece in the long run. These include Hellenism, Orthodoxy, and democracy. Greece is Hellenic by culture and Orthodox by faith; it is also the cradle of democracy. All these are vital for the survival and renewal of Hellenism in the twenty-first century.

It is tragic that Greeks remain politically divided as ever. Greeks were divided during Byzantine times when they faced external threats from the Ottoman Turks in the East and from the Frankish crusaders in the West. Greece was divided in 1920 when Eleutherios Venizelos was liberating Greek populations in Anatolia.

The present Greek government under the progressive Syriza Party is pushing for the secularization of Greece, which is regrettable. Progressive elements in Greece seem to think that democracy is not compatible with Hellenic nationalism and Orthodox Christianity. The truth is that all these things are not only compatible but also represent the foundations upon which Greece should be rebuilt.

Greece has been a functioning democracy since 1974, when the military dictatorship collapsed. For all the problems that have been besetting Greece, such as the West's blatant interference in Greek affairs, Greece did become more stable than it had been. Previous to this, Greek democracy existed under a republic that was established in 1924 by Venizelist army officers and lasted for only eleven years—until King George II gave permission to General Metaxas to impose a Fascist dictatorship on the country. After the liberation of Greece from Nazi rule, a monarchy was established, which in practice intervened blatantly in the political system. It was even alleged that elections such as those of 1961 were stolen.

In 1967, the limited democracy was overthrown by the NATO-backed dictatorship of George Papadopoulos, who was himself overthrown by army officer Dimitrios Ioannides in November 1973.

The political instability and extremism that had been rampant in Greece seemed to disappear after the establishment of a republic in 1974. Tragically, political extremism has returned in the aftermath of the economic crisis. The neo-Nazi Golden Dawn emerged with enough votes in 2012 to be admitted to the Greek Parliament. In 2009, this party had earned less than 1 percent of votes.

For this, PASOK and New Democracy can blame themselves. The return of the extreme Right bodes poorly for the future of Greece, and the establishment of a Nazi Party is to be seriously lamented and mourned by all who value and love Hellenism, Orthodox Christianity, and democracy.

The future for Greece in any case has not been written. But avoidance of a return to the political extremism of the past necessitates a revival of liberal Greek nationalism and the strengthening of the Orthodox Church as the guardian of the nation's morality and conscience. Both major political parties in Greece have abandoned Greek national interests. Consider the failure of Athens to support Cyprus when the Bush administration and the Blair government sought to impose the UN plan of Kofi Annan on Cyprus.

Greece needs to reestablish the purpose of its existence as a nation-state. Greece was established as a state for the Hellenic people, who maintain common language, ancestry, and heritage. One might argue that all countries are established on the basis of language, ancestry, and heritage. The difference between Greece and other countries is that the

Greek leadership has traditionally placed its interests in the hands of the great powers, who disregarded Greece's rights.

It is not unreasonable to expect that Greece should be permitted to pursue its national interests and to insist that its Western "allies" respect those interests. As it stands, Greece needs to reassert its sovereignty and its independence. The internationalism that defined the governments of the nineties and the lunatic military dictatorship of 1967 shared one important trait: the blatant submission to NATO and America and the disregard for the interests of Greece.

The late Prime Minister Eleutherios Venizelos stands as modern Greece's greatest statesman. Venizelos presided over the liberation of Macedonia, Epirus, and Crete from the Ottoman Empire and proceeded to liberate portions of Asia Minor until his downfall from power. Venizelos was not only a liberal but also a strong nationalist and proved that democracy and nationalism are in fact compatible. Venizelism must be the political model for the rebuilding of Greece.

According to Herbert Adam Gibbons in his biography of Venizelos published in 1920, before the Greek elections, "For if the Cretan lives, and continues to lead, he will accomplish what the greatest Mediterranean islander before him failed to accomplish. He will take possession of Constantinople."

Writing in 1928, Winston Churchill analyzed the subsequent loss of Venizelos in the Greek elections: "There was the pro Ally Greece of Venizelos And the Pro German Greece of Constantine. All the loyalties of the Allies began and ended with the Greece of Venizelos." Churchill went on to write about the return of King Constantine after the departure of Venizelos: "The Return of Constantine therefore dissolved all Allied loyalties to Greece and canceled all but Legal obligations."

Writing from Athens in the aftermath of the Turkish military victory at Smyrna and the slaughter of Greek and Armenian Christians, the former American consul general to Smyrna, George Horton, wrote to the State Department, "Another thing that has greatly handicapped the Greeks is their pernicious and corrupt politics. The amount to which politics is played in Greece and the extent to which the Greek Politician will go, even to the sacrifice of his country and of many lives in order to keep his party in power for a few weeks can hardly be believed. The overthrow of Venizelos, Greece's great advocate in Europe and America, and the bringing back of Its discredited King, was the beginning of the end."

This last analysis by George Horton is tragically descriptive of present-day Greek politics as well. Greek partisanship in 1920 led to the downfall of Prime Minister Venizelos, which triggered the isolation of Greece and the subsequent victory of the Turks in Asia Minor after the Western powers abandoned Greece for Turkey.

The point in all this is that Venizelos was a great international statesman who was respected by the West while simultaneously winning support for Greek rights. Venizelos represented a very brief period in modern Greek history in which Greece and the West were genuine allies and Greek interests were properly recognized and supported.

Modern Greek nationalism has been traditionally referred to as the Megali Idea (or Great Idea). The Megali Idea arose during the thirteenth century, when Constantinople was occupied by the Western crusaders. According to Professor Apostolos Vacolopoulos in his *Origins of the Greek Nation*, "Greek nationalism therefore began to assume a more definite form during the period of Latin conquest." Further on he writes, "If Greek Nationalism was born under Foreign occupation, it was nourished by the increasing consciousness of past Greatness which appeared simultaneously in the Empire of Nicea." The Empire of Nicea was the seat of the exiled Greek government.

Nationalism and the Megali Idea were reawakened after the Ottoman conquest of Constantinople in 1453. Following the establishment of modern Greece in the nineteenth century, the Megali Idea was personified by the pursuit of modern Greece to bring about the unification of all Greek-speaking regions within the Ottoman Empire that had remained unredeemed.

The dual liberal and nationalist policies of Venizelos are themselves the continuation of the values of nineteenth-century independent Greece. This work has been critical of the Western role in independent Greece after the achievement of Greek independence, but this does not mean that the West did not do some good things. Greece was given a liberal constitution and was democratic, and there was some good done for Greece by the West.

Venizelos rightfully wanted to abolish the monarchy, which was a foreign institution imposed on Greece. The Megali Idea that Venizelos attempted to bring about is not possible today. In the realm of Greek foreign policy, however, Venizelos and his policies can still be viewed as a model for Greece.

If Greece is to be a partner of the West, it must become so on the basis of mutual respect and consideration for Greece's interests. One common feature of the era of Venizelos and the present is the defection of Turkey. In 1914, the Ottomans backed the Germans while today's Turkey is a de facto ally of the Islamic State. A recent report from Columbia University documents the extent to which the Islamic State has been assisted by Ankara.

With Turkey having defected from NATO, the opportunity exists for Greece to emerge as a significant strategic player, as it was in the two world wars. If the West would recognize that it is in its own interest to support Greece over Turkey and that the Turkish occupation of Cyprus is a threat to international peace and stability that must be ended, then there could be a democratic alliance between Greece and the West.

Unfortunately, there is no one in Greece with a Venizelist-type vision today, and Greek nationalism is not taken into consideration by Greek policy makers. For example, former Prime Minister Costas Simitis, who ruled from 1996 through 2004, was a staunch internationalist. The interests of Greece with regard to national rights against the encroachments from Turkey in Greek territorial waters in the Aegean Sea and the Turkish occupation of Cyprus were not priorities in his administration. The policies of Mr. Simitis were based on the interests of the European Union and not Greece. We have seen how Mr. Simitis fought with the Orthodox Church because he was attempting to impose European demands on Greece without concern for the sensitivities of Orthodox Greeks and their history.

Mr. Simitis also lifted the veto on Turkish entry into the European Union in December 1999. From the time that Greece became a member of the then European Community in 1981, all Greek governments placed a veto on Turkish membership. This was the most efficient means that Greece had to support Cyprus against the Turkish occupation. Greece also placed the veto on Turkey's candidacy in response to Turkish aggression in territorial waters that are part of Greece under the international law of the sea and in order to support the few remaining Greek Orthodox inhabitants living in Constantinople and the islands of Imbros and Tenedos.

Although Turkey did not make a single concession on any of these major issues, Mr. Simitis and his foreign minister, George Papandreou, lifted the veto on Turkey's candidacy, and while Turkey did not become a full member (and probably will not), Ankara moved significantly closer to joining, thus providing the Turks with no incentives to make any concessions toward Greece and Cyprus.

The primary interest of Hellenism in the twenty-first century is to recover its sovereignty and to protect the regions where Greek populations continue to live outside of Greece proper. The populations affected include not only the Greeks of Constantinople but also the large Greek population of Northern Epirus in Albania, which continues to face persecution by the Albanian government without discernible protests from any Western government.

In the aftermath of the Greek genocide, which culminated with the destruction of the Greek populations of Asia Minor in 1922–23, Greece needs to protect Greek populations such as those of Northern Epirus and Cyprus. Persecuted Greek populations have never been on the agenda for NATO, the European Union, or the United States.

Greece's democracy needs not only an improvement in the economy but also a reevaluation of the manner in which its foreign policy is conducted. Greece needs to reassert its rights in national interests, and the West needs to support Greece.

Take, for example, the issue of Macedonia. Macedonia is culturally and historically Greek. Alexander was Greek. Classical scholars attest to this. Yet Slavic chauvinists in Skopje, part of the former Yugoslavia, have sought to usurp the whole heritage of Macedonia. They have built statues of Alexander even though the Slavs did not arrive in the Balkans until many centuries after Alexander had passed. Slavs have distributed maps showing the Greek city of Thessaloniki as part of their own country.

Slavs have even claimed the Greek Christian brothers and missionaries, Cyril and Methodius, as their own even though these saints were the ones who went off to convert the Slavs to Christianity. Despite all these provocations, the West has repeatedly pressured Greece not to oppose Skopje's membership in NATO.

To his credit, former Greek prime minister Constantine Karamanlis (not to be confused with his uncle, the late

Constantine Karamanlis, former prime minister and president who passed on in 1998) resisted NATO pressure in 2008 and vetoed Skopje's membership in NATO. For asserting Greece's rights, Karamanlis made powerful enemies in the West.

A second foreign-policy initiative undertaken by Karamanlis was the establishment of an oil pipeline agreement among Greece, Russia, and Bulgaria. This was later abandoned by his successor, George Papandreou, during his brief tenure as prime minister.

Karamanlis's attempt to bring Greece closer to Russia was a daring display of Greek independence and sovereignty and one that angered Greece's so-called allies.

The Venizelist model recounted above is ideal for Greece—a Greek alliance with the West on the basis of the pursuit of the interests of all parties. Regrettably, Greek interests since the fall of Venizelos have not been respected by the West, and this can be seen in the destruction of Greek populations and Orthodoxy in Turkish-occupied Cyprus and the fact that only two thousand Greek Orthodox remain in Constantinople.

The present situation of Greece is complicated by the West's pressure to keep Greece estranged from Russia. On the one hand, the Western alliance ignores Greek rights and interests, and on the other hand, the West bullies Greece to stay away from Russia. A major problem, as mentioned above, is the advent of the neo-Nazis. This movement has been condemned by the Greek Orthodox hierarchy of Greece, proving yet again that it is the church that is savior and defender of Greece—not the failed politicians.

Mention must be made of the various bishops who have spoken against Golden Dawn. Metropolitan Pavlos of Siatista was among the first voices of the church to speak against racism, and his voice was supported by many metropolitans, including Ignatios of Demetriada, Chrysostom of Messinia, Anthimos of Thessaloniki, Dyonisios of Corinth, and Ierotheos of Nafpaktos, as well as the archbishop of Athens and all of Greece, Ieronymos.

The church has played a stabilizing role in Greek society by providing assistance not only to hungry Greeks during these difficult times but also to the refugees and immigrants (legal and illegal) that have been coming to Greece to escape the war and chaos of the Middle East. As has been noted in this work, the Greek Church preserved the faith of the Greeks and the national consciousness of Hellenism throughout the periods of oppression during the eras of the Frankish occupation and the Ottoman conquests of Greece.

Church-state unity is a necessity for the revival of Greece in accordance with the Byzantine Concept of *symphonia*, or harmony. The Greek people have the right to decide for themselves the relationship between church and state. No one questions the right of Great Britain to have a monarchy. Why should non-Greek interests interfere in the affairs of Greece?

The fact of the matter is that the church is the most Greek of all institutions in Greek society. It predates the establishment of the modern Greek state, and its achievements and role in preserving national identity made possible the Greek War of Independence and independent Greece. The effort by Greek secular parties motivated by pan-European ideologies to silence the church is an attack on Greek independence and traditions. Any attempt to modify church-state relations should be done democratically by consulting with the Greek people and permitting a referendum to be held on the matter. It is the antichurch parties that have refused to debate the issue of church-state relations, as can be seen in the example of former Prime Minister Simitis, who refused to discuss the removal of religion from identity cards but proceeded to act unilaterally without debate.

The late Steven Runciman wrote in his masterpiece, *The Great Church in Captivity*, "It was Orthodoxy that preserved Hellenism through the dark Centuries; but without the moral force of Hellenism Orthodoxy itself might have withered." During the Greek economic crisis, it is the church and its institutions that have been providing assistance to Greeks in need.

As of this writing, Greece has been taking in large numbers of Syrian refugees on a daily basis. This is in addition to the large numbers of legal and illegal immigrants who have been entering Greece for years. The church has been providing support for these people in need as well.

The West seems to perceive that Greece's Orthodoxy is a threat to its own interests. When Greece showed signs that it might be moving closer to Russia, there were hysterical reactions from the West, as if the Western governments owned Greece. We have seen the extent to which Europe and America in the past have exercised excessive influence over Greece.

The refugee crisis that Greece is dealing with is a problem not of its own making. The United States, under the neoconservatives, has destroyed the Middle East, and with the more recent intervention in Syria, its policies have created a humanitarian crisis that the Greeks themselves experienced in 1922, the 1940s, and in Cyprus in 1974. Greeks nevertheless have been performing magnificently, with many Greeks providing shelter and food for incoming refugees. This itself is a sign that the better nature of Greece is manifesting itself.

And let it be remembered that although Greece has not interfered in the Middle East and had nothing to do with the Middle East invasions, the Greek economy is paying a price for the reckless policies of American neoconservatives and their European enablers and collaborators. Germans and others denounce Greece for allegedly demanding money from hardworking Germans and other Europeans, but Greece has not been helping itself to other countries by invading them and overthrowing their governments. In June 2015, Republican presidential candidate John Kasich criticized Greece for even considering accepting assistance from the Russians.

Kasich is ignorant about Greek and Russian issues, but his comments are indicative of the manner in which NATO and Europe continue to seek to maintain control over Greece. Greece's flirtation with Russia is entirely natural and based on self-interest. Greece must survive economically, and the fact that Russia is an Orthodox country strengthens the case for Greek-Russian cooperation.

Russia is the only country that has taken an interest in the Christians of Iraq and Syria who are the victims of the ongoing genocide by the Islamic State. Russian intervention in Syria has been motivated by the desire to protect Arab Christians, in much the same way that czarist Russia fought the Ottoman Empire to protect Eastern Christians under Turkish domination. Ideally, the West and Russia should be working together against ISIS, as they did against the Germans in the two world wars. Unfortunately, the United States and Europe do not understand or appreciate the realities of the Middle East, unlike Russia, who recognizes that existing regimes in countries such as Syria are necessary to counter ISIS.

Greece has a right to survive and to assert her sovereignty. If the West is not prepared to look upon Greece with more understanding and greater respect for Greek interests, then Western leaders have no business pressuring Greece to stay away from the Russians.

Greek politicians deserve a good deal of blame for the present tragedies afflicting Greece, but Greeks do not deserve to suffer collective punishment for the failures of its leaders. This work does not claim to have the answers for Greece's problems, but it is an effort aimed at recalling the complex historical, religious, and political complexities of the past that have contributed to the present tensions between Greece and her Western "allies."

It should not be forgotten that Greece has always supported the West throughout the twentieth century. Mistakes have been made and Greeks are not blameless for the present situation, but readers should be reminded of the German atrocities of the twentieth century. A recent work, *The First Nazi*, by Will Brownell and Denise Drace-Brownell, recounts the German crimes of the First World War that established a precedent for the coming Nazi horrors. Mentioned in this work is the first genocide of the twentieth century: "In their colony in German Southwest Africa, or Namibia, the Germans had started practicing their extermination skills With their fabled efficiency even before World War I."

This writing occurs at a time of political uncertainty. The Paris bombings have occurred, as have the more recent attacks in Belgium. Will the Western world get its act together and reestablish the great alliances of the two world wars? Certainly there is a common interest that should bind the West together with Greece and Russia, and not with an international menace such as Turkey.

At the conclusion of this writing, Greece is still in a state of confusion, with the refugee crisis in the Greek islands and the economic situation still not having recovered. Greece needs assistance, not the overbearing arrogance and lectures of the Germans.

Most of all, Greece needs leadership and a vision, and this may be the most difficult problem for Greece to overcome. On the positive side, Greece has not slipped back into dictatorship and the pre-1974 era. Despite the hits that Greece has taken and the suffering Greece is continuing to endure, Athens remains a bastion of political stability. The Greek Orthodox Church has had much to do with preserving stability and keeping the country afloat. The church's role in supplying food, medicine, and housing for homeless Greeks and refugees alike has been heroic. An example of this can be found in the case of Father Efstratios Dimou. This Greek priest, who died on the island of Lesbos at the age of fifty-seven in September 2015, established an NGO in order to provide for Middle Eastern refugees arriving on the island. He greeted the refugees with blankets and food and provided shelter for them. According to "A Good Samaritan in Greece," an article that appeared on a UNHCR website called Tracks, before the priest's death, "Papa Stratis needs oxygen pumped to his lungs But that's not stopping him from joining the ranks of Greeks helping refugees Arriving in Europe."

A Greece revived without the Orthodox Church is not possible. Consider the example of Metropolitan Chrysostom of Smyrna, who refused to leave his flock when the news of the impending arrival of Turkish victors was apparent. American Consul General George Horton quoted him as saying, "I am a shepherd and must stay with my flock."

The Righteous among the Nations, a tome published by the Yad Vashem in Jerusalem, quotes Archbishop Damaskinos of Athens, who told the Nazis that the Jews of Greece were "the children of our common mother Greece" and that Christianity recognizes "no discrimination, superiority, or inferiority Based upon race or religion."

A fitting way to close this chapter and this work is to cite the comments of Greek Orthodox Metropolitan Pavlos of Siatista in 2012 in response to the violence against illegal immigrants: "My beloved Christians, you have forgotten

Christ's words, 'for as you have done to one of these, the least of my brethren, you have done unto me.'"

Let there be no confusion—what is advocated here is not a theocracy or any sort of church authority over the state. Indeed, canon law prohibits Orthodox clerics from holding public office. Church-state separation exists in point of fact as it did in Byzantium a thousand years ago, if we are talking about administration.

Church and state must be administered separately. Clearly, the church should not have political power. But its historical influence is a fact, as is its contribution to the ongoing Greek struggle. In this regard, it deserves special recognition as the unifier of the Greek nation. In public schools and buildings, icons of Christ and the saints are placed on the wall, and Orthodoxy is taught. The cross is also depicted on the Greek flag, and that is how things should remain.

On the other hand, modernity in some areas is a necessity. There are some Orthodox Christians who believe that monarchy is an Orthodox form of government. This is inaccurate. Byzantium and its monarchical government are long gone, and it is *symphonia*, the Justinian concept of church-state relations, that should be maintained, and not monarchical government. The monarchy in modern Greece was a disastrous failure and came to represent the antithesis of the principles of the Eastern Roman (Byzantine) Empire. As such, Greece must remain a democracy without severing its Hellenic and Orthodox character.

Finally, this work began by referring to the onslaught of anti-Greek attitudes among certain segments of the Western media. For all its difficulties, Greece is still great. Two monastics from Mount Athos have been added to the list of saints of the Orthodox Church. These are Saints Porhpyrios and Paisios, who were glorified in 2013 and 2015, respectively.

Greece is still a place where saints are made. Considering the evils that threaten Greece, including terrorism from without and the threat of the extreme Right from within, Greece needs the Orthodox Church more than ever.

The Future of Greece

———

GREECE'S FUTURE IS CLOUDED AT the present owing to the economic crisis that has been ongoing for over six years. What Greece badly needs is leadership. The best thing that can be said for Prime Minister Alexis Tsipras of the Syriza Party is that he was young and different from the leaders of the traditional parties of New Democracy and PASOK.

During the summer of 2015, Tsipras gambled by holding a referendum on the question of whether to accept a deal offered to Athens by the European Union. Tsipras on the one hand is to be commended for his spirit of defiance, which is lacking among the two major parties in Greece. But he badly miscalculated with regard to the consequences. The people of Greece voted to reject a deal with Europe that would have imposed more painful austerity measures on Greece.

It is here that a serious knowledge and understanding of history would have served the Greek prime minister well.

If Tsipras had recalled the Council of Florence or the 1923 Treaty of Lausanne, he would have anticipated that Greece would face serious punishment in response to the outcome of the referendum of 2015. The awkward relations between Greece and Europe lead one to recall Samuel Huntington's thesis published in *Foreign Affairs* in 1993, which later became a book entitled *The Clash of Civilizations and the Remaking of World Order.*

In the book version, Huntington writes the following:

Greece is not part of Western civilization, but it was the home of Classical civilization which was an important Source of Western civilization. In their opposition to the Turks, Greeks historically have considered themselves spear carriers of Christianity. Unlike Serbs, Rumanians, Or Bulgarians, their history has been intimately entwined with that of the West. Yet Greece is also an anomaly, the Orthodox outsider in Western organizations. It has never been an easy member of either the EU or NATO and has had difficulty adapting itself to the principles and mores of both.

Huntington is to be respected for his honest analysis and critique, if not his viewpoint, which suffers from Western narcissism. It occurs neither to Huntington nor to other like-minded individuals in NATO and the European Union that Greece has serious grievances with NATO member Turkey. Huntington proceeds to argue that Greece has had warm relations with Orthodox Russia and broke with NATO and the European Union over policy toward Serbia during the Balkan Wars of the 1990s.

My response to Huntington's viewpoint is this. The reader must forgive my continued references to the 1955 pogroms in Constantinople, but they were a serious injustice that this author is haunted by. The Greek minority of Turkey was victimized in a Kristallnacht-style pogrom in which Greek churches were burned and desecrated; Greek civilians were beaten, raped, and murdered; and Greek homes and property were destroyed.

One casualty of the pogroms was a ninety-year-old priest by the name of Chrysanthos Mannas, who was doused with gasoline and set on fire by Turkish thugs during the pogrom. NATO member Greece was never supported by any member of NATO, much less the United States, after these horrors. The late political exile and later prime minister of Greece Andreas Papandreou wrote in his 1970 book, *Democracy at Gunpoint*, that "similar acts were perpetrated against Greek Army officers and their families in Smyrna, the location of NATO's headquarters In Turkey. The Greek Army did not react, for it was the American wish that they should do nothing to undermine the alliance between Greece and Turkey."

In 1974, Turkey invaded Cyprus and ethnically cleansed the northern occupied territories of over two hundred thousand Greek Cypriots. Ethnic cleansing of Greeks has never troubled the consciences of NATO or the European Union. Yet Greece is pressured into submission by the West, as can be seen by the infamous letter of Secretary of State John Foster Dulles to the Greek and Turkish prime ministers in the aftermath of the pogroms—which were described as "unhappy events"—where no condemnation or criticism of Turkey was expressed.

The West, then, should not be surprised that Greece occasionally refuses to fall into line with its dictates. Huntington also does not mention within his narrow comments that NATO supported the military dictatorship that seized power in April 1967.

It must be understood that Greece has historical experiences with the West that have been detrimental to the sovereignty of Greece and to the proper functioning of Hellenic civilization and culture, which has suffered horribly at the hands of the Western-backed Turkish leadership in Asia Minor and Cyprus and at the hands of the Nazis during the Second World War. Huntington refers to Greece as the "Orthodox outsider" in NATO. Are the Greeks supposed to abandon Orthodoxy to be Western, something the Franks tried to force the Greeks to do during the Crusades?

On November 25, 2015, Turkey shot down a Russian plane over Syrian or Turkish airspace, depending on whether one believes Moscow or Ankara. The Russians experienced what Greeks have been experiencing for decades, going back to 1922. NATO's failure to repudiate Turkey is de facto tolerance for Turkish aggression. According to the issue of *Forbes* from November 26, 2015, Turkish jets violated Greek airspace 2,244 times in 2014, and up to October of 2015, Turkish jets violated Greek airspace 1,443 times.

Discount the historical horrors perpetrated by the Turks with genocide inflicted on the Armenians, Assyrians, and Greeks. Discount the ethnic cleansing of Greeks from Constantinople since 1955, the invasions and occupation of Cyprus, and the destruction of three thousand Kurdish villages by Turkish forces between 1984 and 1999. NATO and the West have ignored all these crimes against humanity, and the United States still to this day refuses to use the term *genocide* for what happened to the Armenians.

The United States, NATO, and the European Union have ignored Turkey's turn to fundamentalism. As previously noted, Columbia University published a report documenting Turkish support for the Islamic State. The West continues to support Turkey.

What is Greece to do? Greece has to survive. The West demands full support from Greece but has never reciprocated when Greece faced a serious crisis from Turkey or Skopje. As a small country, Greece has been repeatedly pressured to abandon its own interests for the greater good of the West. On the other hand, Greece's leaders deserve blame for their virtual surrender of Greek sovereignty and uncritical obedience to the West. While the German people complain of having to bail out Greece, the Greeks are paying for Western stupidity in the Middle East. Refugees from Syria are making their way into Greece with no end in sight. Who is listening to the grievances of the Greek people who are paying to support refugees fleeing a war that Greeks had nothing to do with?

One is reminded of the 1960 film *Judgment at Nuremberg*, about some of the lesser-known trials at Nuremberg. This film shows the trials of German judges who worked for the Nazi regime and enforced their laws. It is set at the beginning of the Cold War, and there is a scene where the prosecutor, played by Richard Widmark, is told by his superior officer that America will need the support of the German "people," and so it might be time to stop the war crimes trials of Nazis.

Yes, the West needed and needs the German people. Despite the Holocaust and the other abominations of the Hitler regime, Germany has remained in good standing as a Western country. Greece, on the other hand, who was a Western ally in the First World War, whose crushing victories over the Italians helped delay Hitler's invasion of Russia, who heroically resisted the Nazis, and who fought to support the West in Korea, has been completely forgotten.

It is in the West's interest to support Greece and Cyprus at this time. Turkey has completely betrayed the West despite the latter's indulgences for all Turkish crimes and atrocities. If the West were serious about democracy and human rights, all NATO governments would condemn Turkey's human-rights violations, demand a withdrawal of all Turkish troops from Cyprus, and condemn the violation of Greek territorial rights in the Aegean and Greek airspace by Turkey. What is desirable for Greece is to be treated as a genuine partner and ally, not a conquered country. The best example of Greece being treated as less than a fully sovereign nation-state comes from comments made by President Lyndon Johnson to the Greek ambassador in Washington during the sixties:

> Fuck your parliament and your constitution. America is an elephant. Cyprus is a flea. Greece is a flea. If those two fleas continue itching the elephant, they May just get whacked by the elephant's trunk, whacked good...We pay a lot of good American dollars to the Greeks, Mr. Ambassador. If your prime minister gives me Talk about democracy, parliament, and constitution, he, his parliament, and his Constitution may not last very long.

The Johnson comments are mentioned in books by Christopher Hitchens and Peter Murtagh, which are cited in the bibliography. Contrast the insults directed at the Greek ambassador by an American president with the soft attitude for the Nazis depicted in the film referred to earlier, *Judgment at Nuremberg*. Germany is, of course, "Western," whereas Orthodox Greece, as Huntington's comments indicate, is not.

According to Murtagh, Johnson attacked the Greek ambassador because the latter rejected, on behalf of the Greek government he was representing, a "settlement" for Cyprus that would have given part of the island to Turkey and would have ceded to Turkey the Greek island of Castelorizo as well.

The full story and historical trauma of Greece has yet to be told in the West. The story of the slaughter of Greeks and Armenians at Smyrna in 1922 has recently been told in a book by Lou Ureneck, *The Great Fire*. In the aftermath of the massacres, death marches, and exterminationist policies of the Turks, Venizelist army officers in control of the Greek government rejected the humiliating peace that the Turkish mass murderer and war criminal Mustafa Kemal Pasha, with the backing of the great powers, attempted to impose on Greece. According to the Hellenic Army General Staff Army History Directorate, "The Allies realized the Intentions of the revolutionaries and on 16 May 1923 addressed a verbal overture To Greece in which they stressed that, 'The Powers would see a possible operation Of Greece in eastern Thrace with great disfavor and would not allow it to reap the Fruits of a potential success.'"

In the Asia Minor Campaign, the Greeks were barred from defending their brothers and sisters in Asia Minor. When the Turkish slaughter actually ended, the crimes against humanity continued. The Treaty of Lausanne of 1923 permitted the uprooting and expulsion of all Greek Orthodox inhabitants of Asia Minor and Eastern Thrace.

According to the *New York Times* in an article published on January 11, 1923, "In the name of peace and justice 1,000,000 men, women, and children are to be torn from their homes and forcibly taken to other lands. Such was the remarkable decision taken today by this remarkable Near East conference." *National Geographic*, in a 1925 article, "History's Greatest Trek," wrote about what would today be referred to as ethnic cleansing: "Without reference to the total results of the exchange, Greece had received within a year of the fall of Smyrna 1,250,000 exiles."

Historical events take place in a greater context. The realities of Greece today must be seen in their overall historical, political, and cultural context. The Greek people over the last few years have suffered under the imposition of severe austerity measures, leading to the outcome of the referendum in the summer of 2015. That lack of empathy emanating from the German-dominated European Union is a sad repetition of history.

There are positive aspects of Greece's past relations with the West, but they have been certainly exceeded by the negative aspects of Western policies toward Greece. As previously noted, Eleutherios Venizelos represented the best in modern Greece, and his brilliant abilities as a statesman enabled Greece for a brief time to enjoy the benefits of Western support against the brutality of the Turks.

Such a relationship is the ideal that all should hope for. Western democracy is great, as is its emphasis on human rights and international law. Considering the terrible fate that Greeks in Asia Minor, Constantinople, and Cyprus have suffered, it is clear that Greeks have not benefited from the values espoused by the West.

Greeks have been in effect excluded. There are today two hundred thousand Greek Cypriot refugees and their families who dream of returning to the homes from where they were displaced by the Turkish military in 1974. They have no support from the United States or Great Britain.

Greece fully supports the Western values of democracy and international law. It is the unjust and biased anti-Hellenic foreign policy of the West that Greece must reject. A book published very recently from journalist Seymour Hersh makes the following claims about the Obama administration's Turkish policy: "American intelligence had accumulated intercept and human intelligence demonstrating that the Erdogan government had been supporting Jabhat al-Nusra for years, and was now doing the same for Islamic State." Later Hersh quotes a general of the Joint Chiefs of Staff: "Turkey is the problem." Hersh interestingly refers to the Obama administration's policies toward Russia and Turkey, saying "that no anti-IS coalition with Russia is possible; that Turkey is a steadfast ally in the war against terrorism."

One of the final statements in Hersh's book reads, "The Joint Chiefs and the DIA were constantly telling Washington's leadership of the Jihadist threat in Syria, and Turkey's support for it." As it stands, American and Western policies remain firmly pro-Turkish, and this is a devastating threat to Greece and Cyprus. On March 25, 1821, the Greeks declared their independence from the Ottoman Empire. Greek independence, sovereignty, and democracy must be renewed. If the West refuses to recognize the moral righteousness of the Greek struggle and refuses to do what is right by cutting off Turkey, then the Greeks cannot be blamed for pro-Russian sympathies. The spiritual ties between Greece and Russia have been intact for over one thousand years. The two countries are natural political allies.

BIBLIOGRAPHY

Alastos, Doros. *Venizelos, Patriot, Statesman, Revolutionary.* London: Percy Lund Humphries & Co., 1942.

Alexander, John T. *Catherine the Great Life and Legend.* New York and Oxford: Oxford University Press, 1989.

American Hellenic Society. *Persecution of the Greeks in Turkey Since the Beginning of the European War.* New York: For the American Hellenic Society by Oxford University Press, 1918.

American Hellenic Society. *Greece before the Peace Congress of 1919: A Memorandum Dealing with the Rights of Greece.* New York: For the American Hellenic Society by Oxford University Press, American Branch, 1919.

Anonymous. *Inside the Colonel's Greece.* New York: W. W. Norton & Company, 1972.

Bacheli, Tozun. *Greek Turkish Relations Since 1955.* Ontario: Westview Press, 1990.

Bierstadt, Edward Hale. *The Great Betrayal: A Survey of the Near East Problem.* New York: Robert M. McBride and Company, 1924.

Brewer, David. *Greece, the Hidden Centuries: Turkish Rule from the Fall of Constantinople to Greek Independence.* New York: I. B. Taurus, 2010.

Brownell, Will, and Denise Drace-Brownell MPH with Rovt, Alex. *The First Nazi.* Berkeley: Counterpoint, 2016.

Churchill, Winston. *The World Crisis Aftermath.* Norwalk, Connecticut: Easton Press, 1928.

Clogg, Richard. *A Concise History of Greece.* Second Edition. Cambridge: Cambridge University Press, 1992.

Dobkin, Marjorie Housepian. *Smyrna 1922: The Destruction of a City.* Kent, Ohio, and London, England: Kent State University Press, 1971.

Dostoevsky, Fyodor. *A Writer's Diary.* Evanston, Illinois: Northwestern University Press, 1993.

Eastern Orthodox Righteous Among the Nations. Hephaestus Books.

Figis, Orlando. *The Crimean War: A History.* New York: Picador, 2010.

Frazee, Charles A. *The Orthodox Church and Independent Greece 1821–1852.* London: Cambridge University Press, 1969.

Holy Apostles and Dormition Skete. *The Lives of the Pillars of Orthodoxy: Saint Photios The Great, Patriarch of Constantinople, Saint Gregory Palamas, Archbishop of Thessalonika, and Saint Mark Evgenikos, Metropolitan of Ephesus.* Buena Vista, Colorado: Holy Apostles Convent and Dormition Skete, 1990.

Gibbons, Herbert Adams. *Venizelos.* Boston: The Riverside Press, 1920.

Harris, Jonathan. *Byzantium and* Crusades. London and New York: Hambledon and London, 2003.

Hellenic Army General Staff. *A Concise History of the Campaign in Asia Minor.* Athens: Hellenic Army General Staff, 2003.

Helsinki Watch. *Denying Human Rights & Ethnic Identity: The Greeks of Turkey.* New York: Helsinki Watch, 1992.

Hersh, Seymour M. *The Killing of Osama Bin Laden.* London and New York: Verso, 2016.

Hitchens, Christopher. *Hostage to History: Cyprus from the Ottomans to Kissinger.* New York: The Noonday Press, Farrar, Straus and Giroux, 1984.

Horton, George. *The Blight of Asia*. Indianapolis: The Bobbs Merrill Company, 1926.

Huntington, Samuel P. *The Clash of Civilizations and the Remaking of World Order*. New York: Simon and Schuster, 1996.

Hupchik, Dennis P. *Conflict and Chaos in Eastern Europe*. New York: St. Martin's Press, 1995.

Ihrig, Stefan. *Ataturk in the Nazi Imagination*. Cambridge: The Belknap Press of Harvard University Press, 2014.

Katris, John A. *Eyewitness in Greece: The Colonels Come to Power*. St. Louis, Missouri: New Critics Press, Inc., 1971

Koumakis, Leonidas. *The Miracle: A True Story*. Athens: 1996.

Markides, Kyriakos C. *The Mountain of Silence*. New York: Doubleday, 2002.

Morgenthau, Henry. *I Was Sent to Athens*. Garden City, New York: Doubleday, Doran, & Company, Inc., 1929.

Murtagh, Peter. *The Rape of Greece*. Great Britain: Simon and Schuster, 1994.

Nicol, Donald M. *The Last Centuries of Byzantium, 1261–1453*. London: Hart Davis, 1972.

Nicol, Donald M. *The Immortal Emperor: The Life and Legend of Constantine Palaiologos, Last Emperor of the Romans*. Cambridge: Cambridge University Press, 1992.

Norwich, John Julius. *Byzantium: The Early Centuries*. New York: Alfred A. Knopf, 1989.

Norwich, John Julius. *Byzantium: The Apogee*. New York: Alfred A. Knopf, 1992.

Papandreou, Andreas. *Democracy at Gunpoint: The Greek Front*. New York: Doubleday & Company Inc., 1970.

Runciman, Steven. *The Eastern Schism*. Oxford: The Clarendon Press, 1955.

Runciman, Steven. *The Fall of Constantinople, 1453*. Cambridge: Cambridge University Press, 1965.

Runciman, Steven. *The Great Church in Captivity*. Cambridge: Cambridge University Press, 1968.

Speake, Graham. *Mount Athos Renewal in Paradise*. New Haven, Connecticut: Yale University Press, 2002.

Ureneck, Lou. *The Great Fire: One American's Mission to Rescue Victims of the Twentieth Century's First Genocide.* New York: Harper Collins Publishers, 2015.

Vacalopoulos, Apostolos E. *Origins of the Greek Nation, 1204–1461.* New Brunswick, New Jersey: Rutgers University Press, 1970.

Vander Kiste, John. *Kings of the Hellenes 1863–1974.* Phoenix Mill. Alan Sutton Publishing,1994.

Venizelos, Eleutherios K. *Greece in Her True Light Her Position in the World-Wide War.* Translated and published by Socrates A. Xanthaky and Nicholas G. Sakellarios. New York: 1916.

Vryonis, Spyros. *The Mechanism of Catastrophe.* New York: Greek Works.Com, 2005.

Woodhouse, C. M. *The Rise and Fall of the Greek Colonels.* New York: Franklin Watts, 1985.

Yannaras, Christos. *Orthodoxy and the West: Hellenic Self-Identity in the Modern Age.* Translated by Peter Chamberas and Norman Russell. Brookline, Massachusetts: Holy Cross Orthodox Press, 2006.

Articles

"Columbia University Researchers Confirm Turkey's Links to ISIS." *The Armenian Weekly*. November 24, 2015.

"Church Takes Stand against Far Right." *Ekathemerini*. October 29, 2012.

"Turkish Jets Violated Greek Airspace over 2,000 Times Last Year." *Forbes*. November 26, 2015.

"Cyprus Archbishop Asks Russian Church to Help Wrench the North from Turkey." *Interfax*. June 8, 2012.

"History's Greatest Trek." *National Geographic*. November, 1925.

"Greece and Turkey Alert Forces as Tension Builds on Oil Search." *New York Times*. March 28, 1987.

"Greece Treated Like a Hostile Occupied State." *Telegraph*. July 13, 2015.

Internet Sources

Kampmark, Binoy. "The Occupation of Greece: A Financial Coup d'État." Counterpunch.org, July 14, 2015. http://www.counterpunch.org/2015/07/14/the-occupation-of-greece-a-financial-coup-detat/.

Chrysopoulos, Phillip. "OECD: Greeks Are Hardest Working People in Europe." *Greek Reporter*.Com, April 21, 2015. http://greece.greekreporter.com/2015/04/21/oecd-greeks-are-hardest-working-people-in-europe/.

Ledmen, Stephen. "Banker Occupied Greece: Requiem for a Failed State." Counterpunch.org, July 17, 2015. http://www.counterpunch.org/2015/07/17/banker-occupied-greece-requiem-for-a-failed-state/.

"Archbishop Ieronymos of Athens Thanks the Russian Orthodox Church for Her Aid to the Greek Orthodox Church." *Pravoslavie*, November 26, 2012. http://www.pravoslavie.ru/english/57749.htm.

Marshall, Andrew Gavin. "Blaming the Victim: Greece is a Nation Under Occupation." Dissidentvoice.org, July 17, 2015. http://dissidentvoice.org/2015/07/blaming-the-victim-greece-is-a-nation-under-occupation/.

"Skopjan Propaganda #11." History of Macedonia (website), March 14, 2007. http://history-of-macedonia.com/2007/03/14/big-greek-lie-11-saint-cyrill-and-methodios-are-greek/.

"Moscow Wants Turkey to Return Cathedral of St. Sophia to Orthodox Church." Religious Information Service of Ukraine, November 26, 2015. http://risu.org.ua/en/index/all_news/world_news/61791/.

Spindler, William. "A Good Samaritan in Greece." UNHCR. July 6, 2015. http://tracks.unhcr.org/2015/07/a-good-samaritan-in-greece/.

"The Holocaust Martyrs and Heroes Remembrance Authority." From Website of the Righteous among the Nations Department. Greece. Yadvashem.org.